MY LIFE
FROM YUGOSLAVIA TO AMERICA

STANKA JOVANOVIC

Design and Layout: Marina Jovanovic Davis

Published by: DJ Publishing, 325 SE 50th Avenue, Portland, OR 97215

First Printing: April 2005
Second Printing: February 2009
Printed in USA
ISBN 978-0-9796342-0-8

TO MY HUSBAND,
MY DAUGHTERS, AND
MY GRANDCHILDREN.

ACKNOWLEDGMENTS

I am very lucky that I have my brother, Mihailo (Misa) Dimitrijevic, who still lives back home in Belgrade, in the former Yugoslavia, now called Serbia-Montenegro. Misa has spent an enormous amount of time doing research for me for both of my books, *My Life in Yugoslavia* and *My Life in America*. When I asked a question he would go through family documents, inquire at various city and newspaper archives, talk to historians and other experts, and would talk to friends that may remember what we forgot. Misa, being a lawyer, has to do everything in a thorough and systematic way, so that all the facts I have used have been double-checked and are correct. Miso, I love you and I thank you. The good thing is that your children will benefit from these volumes as much as mine will.

I also thank my good friends Marge Bardeen, Jane Brown, Jean Nikolic, Elizabeth Lundy, Junette Gillespie, Phoebe Baron and Eva Clark for reading one or both draft manuscripts, correcting my spelling and my grammar, and for making useful editorial suggestions.

My thanks also go to LaMargo Gill for her final edit of *My Life in Yugoslavia*, and to Derek Van Ittersum for his final edit of *My Life in America*.

Marina Jovanovic, my wonderful niece and a talented graphic designer, did a superb layout and design job and produced this great-looking book. I truly appreciate her dedication to this project. Thank you, Marina.

PREFACE

My Life in Yugoslavia was written in 2003. Many of my family and friends already have a copy or have had an opportunity to read it. After I finished writing *My Life in America* I decided that both volumes belong together representing my whole life. So, here they are printed as one book. I hope that you will enjoy reading it.

Stanka Jovanovic

CONTENTS

BOOK I

MY LIFE IN YUGOSLAVIA

1931–1956

STANKA JOVANOVIC

INTRODUCTION

I recently wrote an article on the early history of Friends of Fermilab, an organization I was instrumental in creating twenty years ago. To my surprise, I could not recall important names and dates and had to look them up. This made me realize that there is no place to look up people and events important in my own life. So, I decided to write my biography while I still remember most of it. My purpose is to record a life that my children, and maybe grandchildren, may be curious about. Life moves so fast and I personally could not be bothered to think and talk about it. As a result, my daughters Jasna and Vesna believe that my life was not a happy one, which, of course, is total nonsense. I grew up in a large, extended family, where love freely flowed. I was a happy child, even though my mother left us when I was five years old. I barely noticed, since my grandfather's household, where we lived, was full of other loving women.

My life happened, sort of, in chunks of years: Prewar, World War II, my high school and university years in the Postwar Communist era, moving to America, and then graduate school years. Then came different phases of my professional life: University of California San Diego, Argonne National Laboratory, and Fermi National Accelerator Laboratory. Then there was the Downers Grove Junior Music Association, which I was instrumental in organizing. And then, most important of all, motherhood.

Altogether I had a very busy life with little room for personal time. Retirement is now giving me that. I listen to jazz, read romance novels and other happy literature. I sit on the sandy beach in front of our condominium on Hutchinson Island in Florida and enjoy the ocean. I sit on our deck in Driggs, Idaho, and enjoy the Grand Tetons. Our home in Urbana, Illinois, is two blocks away from Matejas and Lukas, our most wonderful grandsons. Our older daughter, Jasna, and her husband, Tom, are there too. And, thanks to our need for knee and hip replacement surgeries, we have a perfect excuse to stay with our younger daughter, Vesna, for extended periods of time in Portland, Oregon.

What a great life!

April 2003

PROLOGUE

It is important to note that what I write here is strictly about my life the way I remember it. It is not a historical accounting of the times. Also, due to the fact that when my family moved from Budapest in Hungary to Zemun in Yugoslavia in 1919, they were all adults and their views on many issues and events may have differed from those of people who had always lived in Serbia. Hungarian and Serbian languages were used at home interchangeably. Love for Serbia was paramount for the Serbs living in Hungary. They believed themselves greater Serbs than the "Srbijanci," as they called Serbs from Serbia, the country that was under the Turks "for five hundred years." The Serbs living in Hungary, who escaped the Turks, spent "five hundred years" fighting to preserve their nationality. That somehow gave them a special sense of patriotism. There was also a vast difference between living in Hungary and living under the Turks. Growing up in my family was probably like growing up in two different cultures at the same time. One, that my family brought from Hungary, and the other that evolved while living in Zemun. Sometimes I feel that Drasko, my husband, and I, come from two different countries. Many of his views of history and life in Yugoslavia are totally disconnected from my views. I feel the same way with my other Yugoslav friends. All of them have a true, deep connection to the "motherland," while I have lost any sense of belonging there. This may have made it easier for me to become an American and not be drawn in two directions.

I write this biography for my children, who are familiar with my family, places and the Serbian language. For other readers, I have appended a note to explain the familial terms and the correct Serbian spelling of the names of people and places used in the text. The Dimitrijevic family tree and a map of Yugoslavia with all the places I talk about are also appended.

MY LIFE BEFORE WORLD WAR II
1931–1941

When I was born my parents, Emilija Tabakovic and Milos Dimitrijevic, lived at Nemanjina Street 15, in Zemun, Yugoslavia. I was born at home on April 25, 1931. My brother, Mihailo (Misa), was born a year and a half later on November 3, 1932. We then lived in Belgrade for a couple of years, before moving back to Zemun to live with my grandfather Deda Ceda and grandmother Majka Stanka. My mother left us in 1936, divorced my father, and later married my stepfather, Borislav (Bora) Mihailovic. They lived in Smederevska Palanka. Misa and I stayed with my father and grandparents at Veliki Trg 3 in Zemun.

The main city open market was in front of our house. It was empty in the afternoons and a great playing place. There were other children living in the same building, and we all played together. We played with balls on the sidewalk or played house among the market stalls. We also played house, store, and hospital on the third-floor landing to our building's attic.

Misa and I were enrolled in a German-speaking preschool in 1936. We did not like it there, and we did not last long. One day soon they sent us home. Misa and I undertook to go home alone, probably not realizing that we were to wait for Coka, my father's youngest sister, Sofija. Coka always happened to be at home in Zemun when major events happened in my life. On the way home we stopped to play in the park. By the time we met Coka halfway home she thought we were lost. Feeling sorry for us "orphans," she bought us ice cream at Kod Glumca. Poslasticarnica, a confectionery, was a big store, but we bought ice cream cones at the ice cream cone window. It was inside the big entrance hallway behind the main gate to the building, a precursor to drive-through windows of today.

Later, when Mom started visiting Misa and me once or twice a month, probably as a part of the divorce agreement, we often spent time with her in this same bakery. There were superb delicacies to be had: chestnut puree glazed in caramelized sugar, cream pita, shaum pita, cakes, and ice creams galore. Other times we went to Kej (quay), the big park along the Danube River. We played and watched ships go by. But our favorite pastime was Mom telling us the continuous story about a fat lady, and her amazingly funny adventures. This story lasted until the Second World War interrupted Mom's regular visits to Zemun.

✚✚

I do not remember any vacations with Mom and Dad. After Mom left, Coka started taking us every summer, for a month, to Mojstrana in Slovenija. For several years before WWII, Tetka Beba, Teca Laza, and Ksenija Ilijevic, my father's oldest sister, her husband and their daughter, rented the same house there. They had rooms for guests like us. Mojstrana was in the foothills of the Julian Alps, with Triglav, the highest peak in Yugoslavia, a hiking distance away. I was too little to hike the peaks, but we did lots of short hikes deep into the mountains. I loved hiking a lot, and that love has stayed with me all my life.

We all had bicycles. Our favorite ride was to the Sava River for a day of swimming in the cold, shallow waters of the river, fresh out of the mountain and its spring. The river valley was probably half a mile wide, with white rocks and many branches of azure blue water. It was Coka, Ksenija, Misa, and I who did things together. Tetka Beba was a talented painter, and while we played, she would sit and paint local landscapes. One of these, with Ksenija and me as white dots, now hangs in our house in Driggs, Idaho.

We had so much fun that I do not remember ever missing my mother. My dad never came with us on vacations. He was too busy, or it just was not done in those days. Men worked and did not play. To this day I am very grateful that my aunts, Tetka Beba, Tetka Cicika and Coka, took such great care of Misa and me, not just in those summers before WWII, but throughout our lives. Mom was always a great friend, ready to help with money, but my aunts really worried and took care of us.

Coka was again in Zemun when I started the first grade in 1937. She walked me to school and explained to me why I had to go. I do not remember if I was scared or not. All I remember was that Coka was there, so it had to be okay. The school was in the courtyard of Bogorodicna Crkva, the main Eastern Orthodox Church in Zemun. I went there for a year and then to the Kraljevica Tomislava Elementary School, which was adjacent to a park. It was in the same school building as the German preschool.

I remember three events from those years. One was a class excursion to Zarkovo, a village outside of Belgrade. I do not know why we went there, but I clearly remember that I was the only child who ate in a local restaurant, while all the other children had a picnic on a grassy field next door. Instead of a sandwich, Majka Stanka gave me money to buy lunch. She was probably too busy or did not know any better. This was a small occasion when my life without a mom demonstrated itself, but, I thought I was cool.

I must have been the class treasurer. I had a small matchbox in which I kept the coins I collected. When WWII started, I was suddenly in the possession of class monies and had no clue what to do with them. I agonized, and finally Majka Stanka suggested I go back to the school building and give it to somebody in the office. I must have done it, since I remember being vastly relieved.

After the Germans invaded Yugoslavia in April 1941, I heard at home that they created a concentration camp at Sajam, the state fairgrounds near Belgrade, where they were taking local Jewish people. That did not mean much to me, until one day I heard that two of my 4th grade friends, Mirjana Baumgartner and Blanka Sich, were taken to Sajam. I did not really understand what that meant, but in retrospect, this was a horrendous horror. Even though we were not playmates, their names have stayed with me forever.

++

A major event during 1936 was that I got a strep throat, which progressed to rheumatic fever and then to a heart murmur. Coka's friend, Dr. Jovan Slavkovic, had just returned from Berlin, Germany, where he specialized in heart problems. He put me on digitalis and adigalen. I was on those medications for at least ten years. My understanding was that when my body grew up, it would compensate for the weak heart valve, and I would be okay. This must have happened, since I never had problems later in life.

My heart murmur, still heard today, served me well during the university volunteer labor actions. Under communist rule, students spent summers building railroads. My heart murmur would not allow me to volunteer to do manual labor. I did not complain.

As part of the cure for my heart problem, another doctor took my tonsils out. I vividly remember going with Coka and my father to the doctor's office. There they wrapped me up like a mummy with gauze bandages, put some kind of bridle into my mouth, and cut the tonsils out without any anesthetic. I must have screamed bloody murder, but I do not remember. All I remember is that, for several days after the surgery, I was fed ice cream to keep my throat cool. Today, I doubt that surgery would be necessary.

+ +

In addition to school, Misa and I had private French lessons. We also had music lessons: Misa violin and I piano. There was great music talent in our family, but Misa and I were total duds. Misa had lessons from Petar Stojanovic, Majka Stanka's brother. Deda Pera, as we called him, was a violin professor at the Belgrade Music Academy. He was a known composer and soloist. His time was totally wasted on Misa.

Majka Stanka, my aunts, and Cika Zarko, my father's youngest brother, all played piano and/or violin. Majka Stanka held a music salon often in our apartment in Zemun. I am sure well-known artists participated. Misa and I often eavesdropped and made fun of the performers, especially the soprano singers. WWII wiped out that part of our life forever.

A major occasion in August 1939 was the visit of Aurel and Beba (Benjamin) Haintz, my cousins from Budapest. This was their first visit to their grandparents' home. I remember Majka Stanka was so excited, she bought new white wicker furniture for the den where we children ate our snacks. I do not remember much of their visit, other than that it was an important event.

The boys were Roman Catholics, instead of Eastern Orthodox like the rest of us, which for Deda Ceda was a major tragedy he could do nothing about. In those days, the sons had their fathers' religion, and the daughters, their mothers'. So, Zsofia, not born yet, was Eastern Orthodox. My aunt, Tetka Milica, married Majka Stanka's best friend's son, a Hungarian of German descent, and stayed in Budapest when our family moved to Zemun in 1919. A small detail: after WWII, under Communist rule in Hungary, the Haintz family had to make their name sound Hungarian, so they changed it to Hajto.

++

On April 3, 1938, during Easter vacation, Coka and I were going to our family orchard on Banovo Brdo, on the outskirts of Belgrade. We were to catch tramway 14 (a streetcar) at the Centrala movie theater station in Zemun. At the station, Coka decided to make a phone call before we boarded the tram, and the tram left without us. A few minutes later we heard that a train rammed into that tram at the railroad crossing close to the train station. It was a major accident, but somehow only one person was killed. Thanks to Coka's phone call, we escaped this close call.

Coka must have spent a lot of time in Zemun during school breaks. She was a high school geography teacher in Sombor and had summers off. Going to the orchard during the fruit harvest was always great fun. We had a woman grower who lived in a little cottage in the orchard year around and took care of it. We had red and yellow cherries, peaches and apricots. While there, Misa and I would be up in the trees or on the ladders picking the fruit all day. Cherry harvest was my favorite. To this day, cherries are my favorite fruit.

Sometime during WWII, we sold the orchard, most probably because we needed the money.

For a while, we also owned a lot in Arandjelovac Banja, a spa. Deda Ceda was planning to build a summer home there. WWII took care of that, too. I am not sure when that lot was sold. Majka Stanka and I visited there only once.

Coka was a member of the Belgrade Mountaineering Club. In the early 1930s, the club built a mountain lodge on Avala, a mountain close to Belgrade. Later, the club members were helping with the upkeep of the building, and Coka and I went several times to help out. I have no recollection what I did there, but I felt I did a very important job. Avala had lush green forests and many hiking trails. The big deal was to hike down to the bottom of the mountain to catch the bus back to town instead of catching it up on the top. That distinguished the mountaineers from the sissies, and I was never a sissy!

Zemun sits on the shores of the Danube River. Lido was Zemun's main swimming facility and was located on the Great War Island. When Coka was home, she often took Misa and me to Lido for a day of swimming. We walked one block from home to the Kej, where small ferries were taking people across to Lido. Lido had a beautiful sand beach, large swings, cabins and a restaurant.

The other swimming place on the river was Schwimschule. It was a large wooden platform sitting on multiple drums and was tied to the shore, with two large swimming-pool size wooden baskets sunk in the river. The pools were surrounded by rows of cabins for changing that also gave privacy to the pool area. One pool was for men, the other for women. I think there was also a small, shallow one for little children. The river itself was too fast for swimming. Brave ones could swim in the river by getting into the water at one end of the raft and coming out at the other. If they missed the end stairs, they would have to swim to the shore and walk back to the pools.

++

Deda Ceda was a merchant. He owned a wholesale textile business and had a store in Belgrade and in Zemun. He was also a licensed broker (trgovacki putnik), a business that took him all over the country and abroad. When the first Yugoslav airline, Aeroput, was established, Deda Ceda was their first commercial passenger. He became their most travelled passenger with one hundred and fifty-one flights between 1929 and 1938.

Deda Ceda was a church elder in our Eastern Orthodox Church, Bogorodicna Crkva. As a great patriot and a great Serb, he invested some of his money into recording the church liturgy. The Edison Bell Pencala Company in Zagreb, in Croatia province, recorded sixty-four 78-rpm records called *Rasadnik Srpskog Crkvenog Pojanja*, a collection of Serbian church chants. Laza K. Lera, a teacher from Zemun, sang all parts of the original Karlovacko Pojanje, the authentic liturgy of the old theology school in Sremski Karlovci. The record collection, distributed to churches and schools, never made any money.

In 1956, I brought a complete set of the records to the United States. My father wanted to give it to the Bishop (Vladika) of the North American Eastern Orthodox Church in Libertyville, Illinois. I did visit the man, but after he made a pass at me, I said forget it. So, at my father's advice, I gave the set to a Chicago Serbian youth organization. Dad also gave me a set of seven records with major holiday hymns. In the 1990s, I had them recorded on a tape. I gave the copies of this tape, with the English translation of its contents, to my family and several Yugoslav friends. The records and the tapes are stored in the original Edison Bell Penkala record box, stored in Drasko's closet in Urbana, Illinois.

Traditionally, the oldest son stayed in his father's business. That is exactly what my father, Milos, did. He graduated from a technical textile school in Brno, Czechoslovakia. He then joined his father's yard goods business. It was a very important business since ready-made clothes were not readily available then. You went to your favorite fabric store to buy wool cloth for coats and suits; and cottons, silks, brocades, organza, batistes, terry cloth, etc., for dresses, underwear, linens or towels.

Tailors made men's suits and coats. A seamstress came once or twice a year to our home to make dresses, skirts, and blouses. Majka Stanka, or some other woman in the family, sewed most of the other things the household needed. The Veliki Trg 3 building we lived in had storefronts along its whole length occupied mostly by shoemakers, but, we bought our shoes in the shoe stores.

So, my father worked with Deda Ceda until they sold the business. After that, my dad, with his friend Dragutin-Gaga Cutukovic, started a motion picture import business. They called it Tesla Film located in Belgrade at Kralja Petra Street 26. The office had a small movie theater where they reviewed films they were considering buying. Misa and I loved going there to see films and, if lucky, to meet a movie star. Metro Goldwin Mayer was a customer, and one year Misa and I got a card with signatures of all their stars. Unfortunately, somehow it got lost. WWII wiped out Tesla Film, too.

Coka took Misa and me to see *The Wizard of Oz* at the Centrala movie theater in Zemun. It must have been 1940. It was a very big deal for me, since it was the first color film I saw. I was nine, and Misa was seven. Our favorite movie stars were Judy Garland, Deanna Durbin, Shirley Temple, and Mickey Rooney. I am not sure when I saw *Snow White and the Seven Dwarfs*, maybe later the same year.

For several years before and during WWII, thanks to Dad's film business, Misa and I had free passes to many movie houses. Later, living in Belgrade on the main city square, where many theaters were located, we went to see movies often. Misa developed such a passion for films that after WWII, when he was older, and Majka Stanka was not living with us anymore, he went to see a film nearly every day. For a long time, he kept a diary about every film he saw. He knew who produced and directed it and who played various roles in each film. Actually, after WWII, films were the only windows into the Western world accessible to us.

++

Constancija Stojanovic (Majka Stanka), my father's mother, was born on April 9, 1872, to Constancija (Stancika) Sterio and Evgenije Stojanovic. She grew up in Budapest, Hungary. She had a teaching degree in physical education. In the 1890s, early in her marriage to Deda Ceda, she helped support the family by giving private gymnastic lessons. For a while she was an elementary school teacher in Crepaja, in Banat province, where some of her children were born. Once Deda Ceda became an established merchant, Majka Stanka never worked again.

Majka Stanka's father, although a merchant, was a composer and a patron of the music and literary life of the Serbs in Budapest. Majka Stanka played the piano, while her brother, Petar Stojanovic, educated in Vienna, became a known composer and violin soloist in Belgrade.

Majka Stanka also wrote children's stories. One of them, *Migulac*, was turned into a play Misa and I saw performed at Rodino Theater in Belgrade.

Majka Stanka was the pillar of our family. She was a gentle soul with a will of steel. She kept the household going quietly, and without fuss. We had a maid and a governess. Majka Stanka kept Deda Ceda, a temperamental and energetic man, under control. She closely supervised Misa's and my education, discipline, and play activities without ever having to raise her voice. The harshest words Majka Stanka ever used were "tigar jedan" (you are a tiger). I have no clue why we considered that the utmost reprimand.

It was thanks to Majka Stanka's love and care that Misa and I were not affected by all the comings and goings in our lives. First, Mom's leaving, then Coka's moving to Sombor, changing governesses, and then WWII troubles. In retrospect, Majka Stanka's presence in our lives may have made it easy for my mother to leave us behind after the divorce.

++

I was often asked why my parents were divorced. I really never thought much about it. I was probably too young when it happened, and later it did not matter much. My mother married into a primarily merchant family, a very different environment than what she grew up in. She often told us Misa was the seventh generation of lawyers on her family's side. Her grandfather, Jovan Manojlovic, was a Supreme Court judge in Sarajevo, where Misa and I still own a part of their family home. Jovan Manojlovic and his wife, Emilija Petrovic, had four children. The oldest, my grandmother Olga, married Nikola (Nikica) Tabakovic, a lawyer from Subotica. They lived in Budapest when my mother, Emilija (Baba), later called "Mila," was born on March 8, 1906. From 1905 to 1914 Deda Nikica was a ministerial secretary and then an adviser in the Hungarian government. In 1914 he became an elected representative to the Hungarian Parliament from Velika Kikinda, a town in Banat province. Then from 1921 to 1924 he was the deputy mayor of Subotica, and then from 1924 until 1927 he was the mayor of Velika Kikinda. After Deda Nikica retired the family lived in Subotica. My mom had a teaching degree but never worked.

In 1930, Deda Ceda met my mom on a train trip. He liked her very much and suggested she marry his oldest son. Soon after, a marriage was arranged. The marriage may have worked while they lived on their own. But when they moved back into Deda Ceda's household she probably could not take the extended family life, and left. I do not know why they moved into Deda Ceda's household. Deda Ceda may have ordered my father to do so, or maybe my father could not support his family in the grand style my mother was used to. It is also possible that their divorce was already in the making and that moving in with my grandparents was a good transition for us children. I suspect that Deda Ceda's condition for her to get a divorce was that the children stay with their father, or, better said, with Deda Ceda. At that time Misa was the only grandson with the Dimitrijevic last name, which was very important to the patriarch of the family.

In retrospect, knowing all the players, it was for the best that the marriage broke up while Misa and I were still very young. We were pretty much unaffected and had a great life growing up under Majka Stanka's wing.

++

Our apartment on Veliki Trg 3 consisted of a string of four large rooms that opened one into the other: Majka Stanka's and Deda Ceda's bedroom, a salon that also had Deda Ceda's desk, a dining room with the grand piano, and the children's room. My guess is that the total length of the apartment was at least eighty feet. There was a hallway along the two middle rooms, with a den and the front door on one end and the bathroom at the other. The bathroom was accessed from the dining room and the hallway. The kitchen, maid's room and the water closet were off the hallway. From the kitchen you stepped out onto the balcony overlooking the courtyard. A small balcony off the salon, overlooking the street, was packed with Majka Stanka's plants. The rooms had waxed hardwood parquet floors that Misa and I helped polish by lying on our backs on big polishing pillows and pushing ourselves around with our feet. That was great fun!

Normally, Dad, Misa, and I slept in the children's room. During the three major holidays—Christmas, Easter and Slava—my aunts and uncles came to visit. I have no idea where everybody slept, but I am sure they all stayed with us. The holiday dinners were feasts with several main courses and many desserts. It took days before to prepare everything.

The chickens, geese, suckling pigs, and lambs were bought live, killed down in the courtyard, or on the kitchen balcony, and dressed by our maid. The fruits and vegetables were preserved as they came along during the summer season. Potatoes, beans, and flour were kept in large bags in the pantry. Eggs were stored in newspapers or wood shavings. Fresh milk products and breads were bought daily in the dairy store and the bakery. Pitchers of wine were bought daily at a nearby restaurant. Other staples like sugar and oil were store bought. Noodles and other pastries were made at home when needed. The butcher store in our building supplied fresh meat. Citrus fruits and bananas were imports and very expensive, so we had them on very special occasions, like Mother's Day or Easter.

As far as I can remember, we had a telephone in our home. I am pretty sure this was not a common occurrence in those days. Deda Ceda was the primary user, but others in the family used it too. After WWII, I had a phone in my room I used mostly late at night to gossip with my friends.

For a while before WWII, my dad had a car and a chauffeur. It probably belonged to Tesla Film, but we got to ride in it too. The regular means of transportation in those days were horse-drawn carriages. There was a "taxi" station at the corner close enough to our home at Veliki Trg 3 for us to call from the balcony when we needed one to go somewhere.

WORLD WAR II YEARS
1941-1944

On April 6, 1941, the Germans bombed Belgrade. We all ran to Kej to see Belgrade burning in the distance. Once we realized that we could be bombed too, we spent the rest of the day and the night in our coal and firewood cellar. The next day we moved to a family friend's laundry room constructed of concrete, which, we believed, was bombproof.

Then my grandfather decided that the safest place would be to stay in Francstal, the German part of Zemun. These were native Germans (Folksdeutchers) who, to my surprise, could not wait to have the German army liberate them from Yugoslavia. As soon as it was clear that the country would collapse, the local German youth donned brown shirts with swastika armbands and marched through Francstal. By the time the German army occupied Zemun we were back at home.

A month or so later my grandfather decided it was time for us to leave Zemun and move to Belgrade. By then it was clear Zemun would become part of the new Independent State of Croatia. I do not know how my grandfather, Deda Ceda, arranged it, but his friend, the local police chief, provided us with a horse-drawn wagon (spediterska kola), and somehow we moved all of our possessions to Belgrade.

We first lived in somebody's villa close to the city hospital (Gradska Bolnica) and soon moved to a second-floor apartment at Dobracina 22, close to the center of Belgrade. Later in 1941, the Independent State of Croatia government bought the building, and it became their embassy. We had to move again.

Deda Ceda's good friend, Mihajlo Petkovic, a well-known jeweler and jewelry storeowner, made an apartment available to us in his building at Terazije 1. Terazije was, and still is, the main square in Belgrade. The building was famous for the clock above Petkovic's jewelry store. Later Drasko and I exchanged gold for our wedding rings in that store. I do not remember if we had to pay for the labor. It may have been a favor to us. We were too poor to buy rings, but my family had a gold coin (dukat) we could exchange for rings. I lived at Terazije 1 until I left for the United States in April 1956.

But before my brother Misa and I got to live at Terazije 1, we were shipped off to various relatives, since Deda Ceda and Majka Stanka simply could not take care of us alone. In 1941, I was ten and Misa was eight years old. First, we were both sent to my mother and my stepfather, Cika Bora, in Smederevska Palanka. Cika Bora was a hydro technical engineer and was stationed there. His expertise was taking care of waterways, rivers and canals. We stayed with them for a short time.

Then I was sent to Beckerek (later Zrenjanin) to Deda Ceda's nieces. Misa was sent to Kikinda to Majka Stanka's cousin, Isidora Cenejac, Ivana and Desana's mom. Misa finished 3rd grade there and then returned to Belgrade. I was not very compatible with Tetka Mara and Tetka Juca, the ladies in Beckerek, and they shipped me off to Cika Slavko, their brother in Pancevo.

I was not very happy there, so, pretty soon I packed my things and walked two blocks over to Tetka Beba, Teca Laza and Ksenija's house and moved in. I finished 1st grade and half of the 2nd grade of gymnasium there, and then I went back to Belgrade.

++

All this moving around happened without my father being present. He was a reserve captain in the Yugoslav Army. In 1941, he was activated to fight the Germans. He was captured and became a prisoner of war. In 1942, my dad's three sisters, Milica, Cicika and Coka, petitioned to have him released from the prison camp into their care. All three sisters were then Hungarian citizens, since Pasicevo, where Tetka Cicika lived, and Sombor, where Coka lived, became part of Hungary during WWII. Tetka Milica already lived in Budapest. So, in the spring of

1942, my father was freed and was in Sombor with Coka.

My dad promptly arranged for Misa and me to be smuggled to Novi Sad, then part of Hungary. With a friend of Cika Zarko, my father's youngest brother, we went by train to Novi Becej in Banat province. There a friend of Deda Ceda's placed Misa and me into an indentation on top of a load of hay loaded on a horse-drawn wagon. The German border patrol poked the hay, but did not reach us on top. A ferry carried the wagon across the Tisa River to Becej in Backa province, then part of Hungary.

Then we got on a train to Novi Sad, where Dad waited for us. Another train took us to Budapest. What followed was a wonderful summer, partly in Budapest and mostly in Sejce, a village close to Vac on the Danube River north of Budapest. Tetka Milica and Teca Gena Hajto had a summer home and a big orchard there. Coka was with us, too. She made sure that we had a good time. Aurel and Beba, my cousins, and Misa and I also worked in the family orchard and got paid. We had pocket money, a new concept for us who came from Belgrade. The cousins spoke little or no Serbian, so Misa and I learned a bit of Hungarian. Zsofia and Jeno (Ocsi) were two and four years old, but I do not remember if they were there, too. The Hajtos were vegetarians, even though they were owners of a meat industry plant and a meat products store.

By the fall of 1942, my dad and Misa were back in Belgrade. Dad got an office job with a German company that exported coke (a high-grade coal) from Serbia to Germany. I suspect it was this job that allowed him to come back to Belgrade. I went back to Pancevo where I started the 2nd grade of gymnasium (6th grade in the USA). By the middle of the school year, I was back in Belgrade for good.

We all lived at Terazije 1 with Deda Ceda and Majka Stanka. Our life was pretty much okay. Tetka Cicika managed to smuggle food to us on a regular basis. Once we even got a whole pig carcass smuggled to Terazije 1 by our relatives in Pancevo. For us children that was a special adventure. The over hundred pound carcass was laid out on our dining room table, and a hired butcher dressed it into various parts, made sausages, and melted fat into lard. Most of the meat was smoked or kept in salt brine. Pork chops were fried and stored in lard.

I think it was in the summer of 1943 when the city zoo opened its animal pools for children to swim in. The zoo animals were gone during WWII, so some smart person decided to clean the swans' and seals' pools and let the children in. Misa and I loved swimming there. Normally, Belgrade had many beaches along the Sava and Danube rivers, but I do not remember swimming there during WWII. I also do not remember if we went anywhere that summer. We probably could not.

I guess Misa and I were too young to fully comprehend the vagaries of WWII. We had a good time, and life felt normal to us. And then on Easter, 1944, the Americans decided to bomb Belgrade, and on the second day of bombing, our building was hit.

+++

Who were all these people Misa and I were shipped to? Deda Ceda and Majka Stanka truly could not take care of us, so Deda Ceda called in a few debts. Juca and Mara Ilijevic were his nieces in Beckerek. I believe Deda Ceda provided part of their dowries, thus the debts. Their brother in Pancevo, Slavko Ilijevic and his wife, Julkica, probably also owed Deda Ceda. Otherwise why would they have put up with me? I am sure they were all nice people, but to put up with a ten-year-old child was probably not what they enjoyed doing, and I felt it.

Tetka Zorka (Beba) Ilijevic was my father's oldest sister. Teca Laza, her husband, was an elementary school teacher. It never occurred to me that I could not just move in with them. And I did, and I was at home. The WWII years were very lean, and I clearly remember that Ksenija and I would share an egg for breakfast. Tetka Beba made great yogurt, and with fresh bread, it was my favorite meal.

Teca Laza had chickens in the garden and a pig in the small orchard in the back. They provided the meat. Only horsemeat was available in the stores. We ate that too. You could not buy bread. You had to have wheat grain to barter for bread. I believe the grain came from Crepaja from Ksenija's godparents, old friends of their family.

Ksenija was a high school senior, but did not mind my being around. To this day, I have nothing but happy memories of my life with them. I even got pneumonia during my stay there, and they took care of me. They also made sure I took my heart medicine regularly.

In those days, there was no plumbing in Tetka Beba's house. One of us had to go once or twice a day to the city pump, a half a mile away, to fetch the drinking water. I went often. We had a curved wood rod (yoke) with notches at each end. You balanced the rod on your shoulder with buckets filled with water hanging on each end. I learned how to balance well and never spilled a drop.

For all other purposes we used rainwater. Roof runoffs were collected in a cistern buried in the garden. There were two hand pumps. One was outside, the other in the laundry room attached to the house. We used buckets to keep the water handy in the kitchen. The water was heated on the kitchen stove for washing and dishwashing. We had an old-fashioned hipbath we used for full body baths, maybe twice a month. The rest of the time we washed ourselves in portable shallow basins. All the washing was done in the kitchen. The dishes were washed with hot water, with no soap of any kind, because that dishwater was collected as food for the pig. The dishes were then rinsed twice.

The laundry was washed in two big tubs in the laundry room. In addition, the linen and towels were also boiled with soap in a big copper cauldron in a built-in oven in the laundry room. Tetka Beba made the laundry soap. The laundry was hung outside to dry. There were lines all over the courtyard and the garden. If it started to rain, we would collect the laundry and hang it again when the sun came out. This process may have lasted for two or three days. Since doing the big laundry was such a production, the sheets and towels were changed every three weeks, and the laundry done every six weeks. We washed personal items by hand as needed.

The wooden outhouse was at the bottom of the garden. During the winter, on very cold days, we used a wooden commode in the kitchen. At night, we used chamber pots. We all carried our own pots to the outhouse and then washed them at the outdoor pump.

The house had two bedrooms facing the street, a living room facing the courtyard, a pantry, an entry room, and the kitchen. The wood for heating and cooking was very precious. In the winter the cooking stove in the kitchen was lit in the morning. During the rest of the day, a freestanding iron stove using wood was used to heat the living room. The rest of the house was always cold. Before we went to bed, the doors to the bedrooms were opened to warm up the rooms. I slept on a couch in the living room, while Ksenija, Tetka Beba and Teca Laza slept in the bedrooms.

Rucak, the main daily meal, was prepared in the morning. We ate it early in the afternoon when we came home from school. In the mornings and in the evenings we ate light meals. These were regular eating habits that are still practiced in Serbia today.

We lived on what was then the riverbank of the Tamis River. Our house was on the very first street parallel to the river. We had a terraced courtyard, a few steps down was the garden, and then a low fence separating a small orchard and the pigsty. A tall wooden fence was at the bottom of the property. The back gate led directly to the high water mark shore of the river. The regular riverbed was half a mile away.

Frequent floods brought the river to our back gate. Ksenija had a rowboat, and we had a great time rowing and exploring. In the winter we ice-skated. In the summer we swam in a close-by swimming facility consisting of a gigantic raft with two swimming pool-sized wood crates hanging in the river. In those days the Tamis was clean, and we had lots of fun. By we, I mean Ksenija and me, and her and my friends.

MY HIGH SCHOOL YEARS
1944-1949

On April 17, 1944, the air raid sirens went off in Belgrade just as we were finishing our lunch. The leftover cake from the Easter dinner the day before was on the table. After the bomb hit, the balcony door lay flat on top of the cake. My cat was hiding under the credenza. These are my main memories of that awful second day the Americans bombed Belgrade.

My father and Misa left early that morning to visit father's friend's family in Marinkova Bara, on the periphery of Belgrade to see if we could stay with them to escape from the center of town. When the sirens went off, Majka Stanka and I went to the cellar with all the other people that lived in our six-story apartment building. I remember sitting very close to Majka Stanka in the pitch-black room listening to the booms of falling bombs. Then the big boom came. A bomb hit our building sidewise, demolished the upper two stories and totaled the building next door at Terazije 3.

When all became quiet, somebody peeked through the door to see if we could see the outdoors through the cellar stairway window. The window was completely blocked by debris, but the stairway was clear. So a brave soul climbed the stairs, opened the door to the building stairway, looked through the wire-cage elevator shaft, and saw the sky. But the stairs were intact, at least to our apartment on the second floor.

In the apartment, the windows and doors were all blown in. The frames and broken glass were everywhere. A thick layer of debris covered everything, including the cake on the dining room table. But all that was insignificant compared to our concern for Dad's and Misa's safety. After several hours of agony Dad showed up. He had left Misa with his friends and had come to collect us. Majka Stanka and I packed a few essentials and the cat, and the three of us walked through the devastated town to Marinkova Bara. There were ruins and debris everywhere.

It was clear right away that Marinkova Bara was too close to Belgrade proper. After a week, we moved to Kumodraz, a small village five miles outside of town. There we stayed with a peasant family for a few weeks. Then, somehow we ended up in Crepaja, a village in Banat province, where Tetka Beba, Teca Laza and Ksenija had escaped to from Pancevo. They were afraid that the bridge over the Tamis River would be bombed, and they lived very close to it.

I have not mentioned Deda Ceda in these refugee wanderings of ours. I don't remember his being with us until we got to Crepaja. It is possible that he went to Pancevo to search for a place for us to escape to and was not able to come back to Belgrade.

Once we were safe in Crepaja, Dad stayed in Belgrade and went back to work. The Americans bombed Belgrade several more times until September of 1944. My dad survived all of it. Sometime during the summer, I had to go back to Belgrade to take an exam to complete my 3rd grade of gymnasium (7th grade in the United States). I have no recollection of how I got to Belgrade from Crepaja, but I did. Maybe they just put me on a direct train in Crepaja, and Dad collected me at Dunav Station in Belgrade. The exam was in a churchyard on the periphery of Belgrade. We took a tram there. The teachers sat along a long table. A student sat across from a teacher answering the few questions asked. The exam took only a few minutes. I passed with flying colors.

Our Belgrade apartment was still in total disrepair, but it was clean. The windows and doors were back in place. The big problems were the bed bugs (stenice), roaches (buba svabe) and rats (pacovi). The bed bugs were the biggest nuisance. After the first night I was so bitten, I looked as though I had chicken pox. I think I stayed only a day or two, and was back in Crepaja in no time. While in Belgrade I cooked my very first dinner for Dad and me. I made rezance sa sirom, noodles with cheese. Dad was so proud of me, and talked about it for years.

Right: I am six-and-a-half months old in this picture. Crepaja, *November 11, 1931*

Above: My family: my brother Mihailo (Misa), my mother Emilija, my father Milos and I. Zemun, *January 1933*

Right: My brother Misa and I. Zemun, *1934*

This is the infamous "as-their-mother-left-them" picture taken after my parents separated. Zemun, *1936*

Left: My grandmother Majka Stanka, Misa and I in Belgrade. We are in our new Easter outfits. *Spring 1937*

Left: I am on the way to school on my first day of the first grade. Zemun, *September 1937*

Below: Patron Saint Day (Slava) dinner in Zemun. Our family's patron saint was Archangel Michael. In the picture clockwise are our governess, uncle Zarko and aunt Gordana, uncle Laza, I, my grandfather Deda Ceda, my brother Misa, Aunt Coka, my grandmother Majka Stanka, my great uncle Petar Stojanovic, aunt Beba, aunt Cicika and my cousin Ksenija. *November 21, 1937*

Left: My aunt Coka, my cousin Ksenija and I on our daily bicycle ride in Mojstrana in Slovenia, where we spent many vacations. *Summer 1938*

My father Milos, Misa and I strolling in Belgrade. *October 15, 1938*

I am dressed in a Serbian folk outfit for a patriotic school play on Sveti Sava holiday, Saint Sava Day. Zemun, *January 27, 1940*

My cousins from Budapest, Hungary, came to visit us in Zemun. It was the first time my grandparents had all their grandchildren in their home together. Back to front are: my cousin Ksenija, who came from Pancevo, Aurel and Benjamin (Beba), cousins from Budapest, I and my brother Misa at Kej park along the shore of Danube River in Zemun. *August 1939*

Left: The school picture for my first grade of gymnasium (fifth grade in the United States) that I attended in Pancevo. *September 1941*

Below: During the first two years of World War II, I lived in Pancevo with my cousin Ksenija's family. Ksenija and I took care of the chickens. In those days home-grown chickens were our main source of meat. *1942*

Left: My aunt Coka, my father Milos and my uncle Miska on the day my father arrived in Sombor from the prisoner-of-war camp in Germany. Coka and Miska lived in Sombor. *Spring 1942*

My brother Misa, my father and I. My father's beard was a leftover from his prisoner-of-war days. Belgrade, *1942*

My grandfather Deda Ceda, Misa and I. Pigtails for girls and shaved heads for boys were part of the school dress code in Independent Serbia during the Second World War. Belgrade, *1943*

Right: Drasko Jovanovic, then my boyfriend, and I in Soko Banja, a spa in Serbia where Drasko's family had a summer home. *May 1, 1951*

Above: Drasko and I at Lapad in Dubrovnik, in Dalmacia. *July 1951*

Right: Drasko and I on the summit of Triglav. Triglav, 2864 meter high, is the highest mountain in Yugoslavia. The five-pronged red star on the top of the summit shelter was the symbol of the Federal People's Republic of Yugoslavia. *August 1951*

Drasko's and my wedding picture. We were married in Belgrade on August 8, 1954. Drasko was twenty-four and I was twenty-three years old. A few weeks later Drasko left for the United States to attend graduate school at the University of Chicago. I did not see him again until May 1956.

Left: Branka Todorovic, Anica Jovanovic and I, and Marija Lalevic (below), were wives left behind when our husbands left to attend various graduate schools in America. Belgrade, *Summer 1955*

Below: My father Milos and Marija Lalevic in the Japanese Garden in Philadelphia. My father was on the way back to Yugoslavia after a six month visit with us in Chicago. *April 1963*

This is the last family picture taken before I left for the United States to join Drasko and to attend the University of Chicago Graduate School. In the picture from left to right are my brother Misa, my father Milos, my stepmother Katica, I and my uncle Zarko Dimitrijevic. Belgrade, *January 1956*

My brother Misa, my mother Emilija (Mila) and my stepfather Borislav (Bora) Mihailovic. This picture was taken after I left for America. Belgrade, *October 1960*

Dimitrijevic family picture taken in June 1932. Sitting left to right are my uncle Miska's first wife Maca, my mother Emilija, my grandmother Majka Stanka holding Benjamin (Beba) Hajto, Aurel Hajto, my grandfather Deda Ceda holding me, my aunt Beba Ilijevic, my aunt Milica Hajto; standing left to right are my uncle Miska, my father Milos, my uncle Zarko, my aunt Cicika, my aunt Coka, my uncle Lazar Ilijevic and my uncle Jeno (Gena) Hajto; sitting on the floor are my cousins Ksenija Ilijevic and Marica Jeftic.

My parents', Emilija Tabakovic and Milos Dimitrijevic, wedding picture is the only one that I have that shows my maternal grandparents and my great-grandmother. In the picture sitting from left to right are my mother's father Nikola (Nikica) Tabakovic, my father's mother Stanka Dimitrijevic, my mother's grandmother Emilija Manojlovic, my mother's mother Olga Tabakovic and my father's father Ceda Dimitrijevic. To the right of my father are uncle Miska, aunt Maca, aunt Coka, my mother's sister Marija (Beba) and her husband Bozidar Rakic. Their son Nikica Rakic is in front on the left. My parents were married on July 12, 1930.

I have wonderful memories of my life in Crepaja. First, Majka Stanka let me cut off my pigtails, probably because long hair was hard to wash and manage in our refugee situation. I loved having a light head and loose hair. Second, Ksenija was there, and the family we stayed with had several children close to our ages. I thought village life was great. All the young people participated in the regular fieldwork. We worked in the potato fields, cornfields, wheat fields, and in the vegetable gardens. For lunch breaks we sat under a tree and ate raw cabbage, fresh crusty bread and slices of smoked ham. To this day, I love that food. I was so enthralled with the fieldwork that I decided to study agriculture when I grew up.

We also played a lot. Our favorite pastimes were climbing, playing, and sleeping in a gigantic haystack in the backyard. The Vesin family, the farmers we stayed with, had a three-wing house facing the street. Tetka Beba, Teca Laza and Ksenija had one wing. Majka Stanka, Deda Ceda, Misa and I slept at another farmer's house across the street. In the big yard at the Vesins' house, perpendicular to the house, was a long building with the kitchen, dining area, stables for horses, carriages, plows and such, and then a barn with cows, chickens, and pigs. Along the sides of the yard were other farm buildings. In the back of the yard was a haystack, feed for the animals, and then at the far back was a big vegetable garden. An air-raid shelter, a hole in the ground covered with boards and dirt, was also in the garden. At any given time there were ten or more Vesin family members plus us, which made for a big crowd at every meal, play or any other activity. I loved it. I also remember we went swimming, but I have no clue where. There must have been a canal close by.

This was the summer of 1944, when partisans were very active fighting Germans. They lived in the cornfields, and they would come out at night to burn local German collaborators' homes. We would hear the movements in the street and would watch armed people running through the deep ditch that separated the road from the sidewalk. Then we would see bright light, wherever they started the fires.

By September, the Russians were advancing toward Crepaja and the Germans were pulling out. At one point, a German tank with two soldiers got separated from its unit. Partisans caught them, stripped them, and shot them in the park. Then they tied their bodies to a horse-drawn buggy and dragged them through the village. This was probably the only time when I truly witnessed the horrors of WWII.

In early October, the Russian army finally came to Crepaja. We jubilantly greeted the first unit that came through the village. They came on carts pulled by horses and camels. The soldiers looked ramshackle and not at all like liberators. But for us, WWII was over.

Soon after, Deda Ceda went to Pancevo to organize our return to Belgrade. Instead, he was killed by a brick that fell off a bombed building. It was October 27, 1944, few days after his and Majka Stanka's 50th wedding anniversary. Deda Ceda is buried in Pancevo, close to Teca Laza and Tetka Beba's graves. A week or so later, Majka Stanka, Misa, my cat, our belongings, and I were transported by a horse-drawn wagon back to Pancevo. I don't remember how we got back to Belgrade, but we did get back and I was back in school (4th grade of gymnasium).

++

By the time we came back to Terazije 1, our apartment was repaired and everything looked normal. But the bugs and rats were still present. Majka Stanka, who knew how to do everything—at least I believed—attacked the problem. We spent hours dripping petroleum into every crevice we could find in the wood bed frames. Mattresses, too! A white powder, cockroach poison, was spread along all the walls. The rats had been climbing up along the coal elevator shaft cables onto the kitchen balcony. Then one day there were no more. The janitor must have gotten rid of the rats in the cellar.

At one point I even got lice in my hair, so Majka Stanka soaked a towel in petroleum, and wrapped it around my head. In a day or two, I was clean again. None of this was made into a big deal. We just went along with whatever life we had.

It took a year before we were truly back to a normal school life. Right after WWII, there were too many young people who had to make up for grades lost during the war. There were more students than schoolrooms. So, for a while, we were located in a teachers' college and had classes in shifts. By the 5th grade of gymnasium I was in my regular school building, Second Girls Gymnasium on Kraljica Natalija Street, a few blocks away from Terazije.

The school did become a different place under Tito's communist government. All the subjects, including science, had a dialectic materialism interpretation. History was broken into slavery, feudalism, capitalism, imperialism, and socialism that would evolve into the ideal system, communism. Various revolutions marked the historical boundaries. As a consequence, I know little real history of the world. For example, the Second World War was all about seven German offensives against Tito's partisans, and very little of anything else.

But we had good teachers and we still learned a lot. I was very good in science and math and not so good in Serbian language and literature. I was the first generation in my family that was born in Yugoslavia. My family had escaped the Turkish invasion in the 17th century and lived in Budapest until 1919, when the Versailles Peace Treaty created Yugoslavia. All the great Serbs, including my grandfather, Deda Ceda, moved back to the motherland. But by the time they moved to Zemun, all of his seven children had gone to Hungarian schools in Budapest and never became truly proficient in Serbian written language. As a consequence, I also had problems with language and literature, and still do.

++

My best friends in high school were Mira Danicic, Vera Bojic, and Ljubica Ziskovic. Ljubica's father owned the biggest fancy confectionery (poslasticarnica) in town. It was located in the Serbian Academy of Science building on Knez Mihailova Street, the main street in Belgrade. Much later, probably in the 1970s, the street was closed to traffic, and to this day it is the main promenade in town. We went for walks, stopped at Ljubica's confectionery and ate tons of marzipan, my favorite dessert. Then we continued to Kalemegdan, the main city park on the estuary of the Sava and Danube rivers. The park was on the grounds of the old fort, Kalemegdanska Tvrdjava. It was a place of great historical significance that we took for granted. Our primary goal was always to meet other friends and ogle the boys.

In those days Mira's father, Sinisa Danicic, was my doctor. His office was in their apartment on Poenkareova Street, two blocks from Terazije. We spent lots of time in Mira's apartment. Her mom, Nada, and their neighbor, Nikola Maksimovic, also a doctor, played four-hand piano incessantly. They played all nine Beethoven symphonies, and much more.

Vera's mother owned a beautiful flower shop just down the street from my home. We liked spending time there, too. Right after high school, Vera got married and left Belgrade. Mira started medical school, but quit after the first year. I went on to study chemical engineering. Soon we drifted apart.

Immediately after WWII, probably in the spring of 1945, the high school students helped with work in the farm fields. My class went only once to Bezaniska kosa, an area on the northern shores of the Sava River. During the lunch break several of us walked to the river shore. There we discovered rows of dead bodies, tied together, floating down the middle of the river. A bloated corpse covered with flies was stuck at the shore. We pushed it away and sat down and had lunch anyway. These were corpses from the Independent State of Croatia concentration camps up the Sava River. Apparently they were killing Serbian prisoners as fast as they could before the Russians and partisans came. WWII was still going on in Croatia, a hundred miles or so, west of Belgrade.

++

Sometime after WWII ended, my mother and my stepfather, Emilija and Borislav Mihailovic, moved to Belgrade. They had a very nice apartment on Hadji Milentijeva Street. They had a working water heater in the bathroom, and Misa and I were welcome to take a bath any time we wanted. What a glorious experience that was. I had not had a proper bath since the bomb demolished our apartment's central heating system and we had no running hot water. With the delicious meals, including cakes Mom made, our visits to Mom became frequent. She also frequently came to Terazije 1. She always brought delicacies that Misa and I devoured.

Soon after WWII, Majka Stanka, who was 73 years old in 1945, was spending more and more time with Tetka Cicika in Zmajevo (former Pasicevo), and with Coka in Sombor and Cika Miska, my father's younger brother, in Pacir in Backa province. Dad, Misa, and I lived alone. At some point, Ivana Cenejac, my father's second cousin, came from Kikinda and for a while took care of us. On April 27, 1951, my father married Katica Vasiljevic, and for the remaining five years, before I left for the United States, we had a family life again.

It must have been very important to my family for us children to spend summers away from the big city. From 1945 to 1949, we spent summers at Tetka Cicika's in Zmajevo, at Coka's in Sombor and with Coka in Kranjska Gora, and in Gozd Martuljek in Slovenija.

Tetka Cicika was a kindergarten teacher in Zmajevo, a village in Backa province. She lived in a two-wing house. Two classrooms were in one wing, and her apartment was in the other. Since school was out, Misa and I had the run of the classrooms. Zmajevo had artesian springs that fed three big public swimming pools, a rarity in those days. Few people used the pools, so we and our friends had the pools to ourselves. We had a very nice group of friends, mostly children who had come back home for the summer from the various schools they attended.

Coka was a high school geography teacher in Sombor. Some of her students, primarily her friends' children, befriended me and I had a great time there, too. The canal, Dunav-Tisa-Dunav, was very close to Sombor and was great for swimming. Bicycles were the main form of transportation, and we cruised.

My uncle Cika Miska and his first wife, Maca, also lived in Sombor, but I did not see them often. I think Maca was a sickly person, and soon after that summer she died. They owned a grocery store. Cika Miska later married Eta and became a railroad stationmaster in Pacir, a village close to Subotica. They had two boys, Cedomir (Ceda) and Zlatibor (Bata), who were born in 1953 and 1954. Ceda and his wife, Vukica, and Bata and his wife, Vera, and their children now live in Temerin and Novi Sad, in Backa province.

In 1947 Ivana and I spent a month in Split with her cousin Leonidas-Bata Najman and his family. Split is a city on the Adriatic of major historical significance. The Diocletian Fort is an integral part of the city. For Ivana and me the important daily activity was going to Bacvice, the main swimming beach. There I met and lost my first love. Dragan (I have forgotten his last name), a merchant marine, was gorgeous in his swimming suit, and I was in love. One morning I managed to get to the beach before my other friends were there. I saw Dragan lying in the sand. In my enthusiasm, I ran to him, lovingly kicked him in the ribs and said "hi" with a smile. I must have kicked him too hard. The poor man bent over in pain and refused to talk to me ever again.

Branko Ozretic was another handsome young man. He owned a small sailboat. He took me sailing several times to the little island close to the shore. It was great fun, but I was pining for Dragan and sailing did not move me. In the evenings, a bunch of young people would meet in a garden restaurant where we danced and had fun. I was 16; Ivana was 15 years older.

My vacations in Slovenija were totally oriented to mountain hiking. The highest peaks in Yugoslavia were in the Julian Alps. My goal was to climb as many as possible. The trails were well marked and secured. Triglav, 2864 meters high, was the highest peak in Yugoslavia. I climbed it three times at various times in my life. The main trailhead was in Mojstrana at the altitude of about 1000 meters.

Early on I hiked with Coka. Soon afterwards I joined the Radnicki Mountaineering Club in Belgrade. The club had many organized hikes, and I went often. Once, hiking in the Alps, I recognized Coka's backpack in one of the mountaineering huts where we stopped to rest and eat. Coka went on a hike and left her backpack in the hut to pick it up on the way back. I decided her backpack was better then mine, so I repacked and left mine for her to find. Coka thought that was very clever of me. Coka never got mad with Misa and me, and we dearly loved her until the day she died in September 1992. She was 87 years old.

In January 1949, Mira Danicic and I traveled alone to Slovenija to have hiking boots made for us by a well-known cobbler in Mojstrana. We stayed in Kranjska Gora while waiting for the boots to be made. The countryside was covered with snow, but the weather was sunny and pleasant. And, of course, we did lots of hiking. On top of Mojstrovka mountain, we met Bora Damic, who, for a while, became Mira's serious boyfriend. Their relationship did not work out. He was a Roman Catholic, and Mira's family simply did not allow her to marry outside of our Eastern Orthodox religion.

The other interesting thing was that I left Belgrade with a bad cold, and Dr. Danicic, Mira's dad, who came to the railroad station to see us off, gave me a dose of penicillin to take. That was the very first time I heard of antibiotics, and they worked. I was perfectly healthy throughout our mini-vacation.

I also had a sad experience that summer. Igor from Slovenija joined our Radnicki Club group for a ten-day hike through the Alps. We climbed Triglav and several other peaks. We hiked from one mountain hut to another, and did not come out of the mountains during the whole trip. Igor and I became good friends and had a great time together. We were going to continue our friendship long distance after we returned home. Unfortunately, Igor was soon diagnosed with leukemia and died. It was the first time in my life that a close friend of mine died.

Throughout my life, vacations were very important to me. Sitting on a beach, or hiking the high mountains, was the ultimate. Today, owning our house in Driggs in Idaho, and our condo on Hutchinson Island in Florida, is the crowning glory of all our vacations.

++

We went to school six days a week from 8 a.m. to 2 p.m. I don't remember how much homework we had, but I must have done it in the afternoons, since the evenings were always busy with fun. The main activity was meeting friends on the korzo, the main promenade in Belgrade. It stretched from Hotel Balkan on Terazije, across the street from my apartment, all the way to Kalemegdan Park. Different groups of friends had designated meeting spots along the route. Usually these were a telephone pole or a tree. Many times we did nothing but walk from one end to the other, sort of like a very long parade that folded back on itself. This way we faced other friends walking back, and we could stop to gossip or change groups.

The other major evening activity was going to the opera. The opera was housed in the National Theater (Narodno Pozoriste) one block from my house. The top balcony was standing only, and I believe free for students. We also knew ushers who may have let us in free. I don't remember ever paying in those days. I saw every opera that was performed, including *Porgy and Bess* performed by a visiting group from the United States in December 1954.

We also went often to Kolarcev narodni universitet, where Belgrade's main concert hall was. There I heard, among many different concerts, *Carmina Burana* and a group of American black women singing spirituals. Both performances were exotic to me.

We went to see drama performances at the Theater at Vracar (Pozoriste na Vracaru). Ballet was housed in the National Theater.

And, of course, we went to movies very often. The first two films I saw after WWII were *Pygmalion* with Leslie Howard and *Bathing Beauty* (Bal na Vodi) with Esther Williams and Red Skelton. *Bathing Beauty* opened a whole new world for me of swimming pools, jazz, gorgeous swimming suits and lush life.

Tito and his socialist regime did not approve of decadent bourgeois living, so we did not see many new movies from the Western countries. We were served a healthy dose of morbid Soviet war movies.

Belgrade had a beautiful public library close to Kalemegdan Park. I often walked by it but never entered it. Public libraries were for poor people. Families like mine had their own book collections. If you did not have the book you wanted to read, you bought it.

Mira Danicic's family had complete collections of classic authors that I was allowed to borrow from. Thanks to them I have read many works of French, Russian and English authors. I also read Karl Maj, a German author who wrote novels about the American West. I loved them. Karl Maj wrote them while in jail. He never visited America. Later I learned that none of my friends in the United States had ever heard of him. I also read many Yugoslav authors and many children and young adult books.

At some point in the late forties, Belgrade bookstores were flooded with American paperbacks. They were cheap, and I spent all my pocket money buying them: John Steinbeck, Tennessee Williams, Hemingway, Sinclair Lewis, Upton Sinclair, and others. There were also series of murder stories by Agatha Christie and many others. I read incessantly. Reading was then what television is today.

++

Terazije 1 building was a set of four buildings one behind the other—two and two—connected by a stairwell. Our apartment was on the second floor in the second building of the first set. Two connected big rooms were facing two courtyards. Misa's and mine was the third big room, an extended L facing the second courtyard. There was a hallway along the two rooms, with the entrance on one end and Misa's and my room on the other. The bathroom, water closet, kitchen, a maid's room, and a pantry were off the hallway. We had a kitchen balcony with an elevator shaft that brought coal and wood from the cellar. There was also a nice size balcony off the dining room overlooking the second courtyard.

For several years after WWII, we rented the first room to two students, providing much needed extra income for the family. At that time Majka Stanka was spending more and more time away from us. My dad slept in the dining room, where we had three single beds, and Misa and I slept in our room, with two single beds. We also had an extra bed in the hallway. Our guests, and we always had somebody visiting, slept all over the place. It was pretty common in those days to have unrelated people sleep in the same room.

My uncle Zarko lived in Belgrade with his wife Gordana's family. Soon after WWII his father-in-law, Prota Antonije Osmec, an Eastern Orthodox priest, was transferred to the church in Trieste, Italy. In 1951, Strina Gordana went to visit her parents in Trieste and never came back to Belgrade. Eventually she moved to New Haven, Connecticut, where her sister was married to a professor at Yale. Zarko and Gordana divorced several years later, and eventually they both remarried. After Strina Gordana left for Trieste, Zarko was alone in his apartment in Dositejeva Ulica. He invited Misa to stay with him until Strina Gordana returned. Misa did, and our room on Terazije became mine alone. I loved it.

✠

Terazije 1 building had a laundry room on the sixth floor. There was also a partly covered terrace to hang the laundry. A laundry woman came every six weeks and spent three days doing the big laundry, including ironing. In the winter the laundry would freeze-dry into rigid sheets that I loved collecting and crushing into the laundry basket.

I do not remember if there were ready-made clothes in the stores. A seamstress came regularly to our apartment to make stuff for all of us. Once in a while we bought used clothing from people who received packages from relatives in America.

Tetka Beba in Pancevo, and my mom's best friend Milka Milojevic in Belgrade, also made clothes for me. Tetka Milka made great swimming suits. Tetka Milka's daughter, Beba, married to Dragan Todorovic, now lives in Toronto, Canada. They own a house in Stuart, Florida, very close to our condo on Hutchinson Island. We often see them there.

✠

Right after WWII, my father worked at a wholesale food company. When a truck loaded with fresh meat got stuck somewhere on the road to Belgrade and the meat was spoiled, my father was held responsible. He was sentenced to six months of prison labor. For a few weeks he shoveled coal at the Belgrade power plant. Then he was transferred to the Belgrade militia's food warehouse as a bookkeeper.

After his sentence was over, he stayed as an employee of this closed-type food store. The store distributed free food to the members of the Belgrade militia (police). As an employee my father also received free food. I remember Misa and I going with a big laundry basket to collect our rations of food. It was free and of good quality. It eased our financial problems a lot. Later when the closed stores were abolished, the company (Vracar) became one of the biggest wholesale food companies in Belgrade. My father stayed with them until he retired.

MY UNIVERSITY YEARS AND
LEAVING FOR AMERICA
1949–1956

My physics teacher during my senior year of high school (8th grade of gymnasium) was an old college friend of Dragoljub K. Jovanovic, Professor of Physics at the University of Belgrade. As a favor to her, Professor Jovanovic was going to come to our school to give a lecture on modern physics. On the appointed spring day in 1949, instead of Professor Jovanovic, his son Drasko showed up. Drasko brought a number of instruments and proceeded to impress us girls with various measurements of sound, electricity, and such. Drasko was also a high school senior, and in my mind had no business giving lectures to his peers. It was clear to me that the poor soul had no life, and I felt sorry for him.

A few weeks later, I was taking my entrance exam at the Department of Chemical Engineering at the University of Belgrade (Tehnicki Fakultet). After I finished my exam, I went to the Department of Electrical Engineering to wait for a friend who was taking her entrance exam there. Who was there already waiting? Drasko. I was so flabbergasted to see him in the College of Engineering building that I promptly asked him why he was not in the liberal arts building registering to study physics. Drasko was taken aback by my direct attack and defensively told me that he was also waiting for a friend. Later, he told me that he actually came back to my building to see the posted results of my entrance exam. He was properly impressed that I passed.

As a member of the Belgrade Mountaineering Council, I was in charge of the mountaineering equipment and clothing the government was providing for the mountaineering clubs. All sports were government subsidized, and included very cheap train travel, which enabled hikers to get to the mountains in large numbers. One day in early summer, to my great surprise, Drasko, representing his Slavija mountaineering club, showed up at my door to pick up his club's share of the supplies. He promptly discovered that my doorbell did not work and offered to come some other time to repair it. I said fine. A few days later he came and fixed it. He also invited me to go with him on a hike to Topcider, a hill within the city limits. A few more hikes followed. Then I invited him to the New Year's party in my apartment, and the rest is history.

After my first year as a chemical engineering student, I was informed that Tito decreed that a new Department of Metallurgical Engineering be created. The university transferred the top twenty chemical engineering students to the new department. I was one of them. I did not even know what metallurgy was and had no recourse of any kind. You did as you were told. Drasko tried to pacify me by convincing me that physical metallurgy was close to physics, so we would have something professional in common. It turned out that the study of metals from ores to finished products was fun and I loved it. Later, my knowledge of physical metallurgy served me well, both in my job at the Metal Institute at the University of Chicago and later in my lunar and meteorite research at Argonne National Laboratory.

The college years were very hard. We had classes from seven in the morning until one in the afternoon, and the labs from one in the afternoon until seven in the evening. We probably had fifteen-minute lunch breaks. It was like this for eleven semesters, five and a half years. In addition, I had to produce a thesis to get the B.S. in Engineering. Professor Branko Bozic, my department head, who taught iron and steel metallurgy, suggested I talk to Professor Dragoljub Jovanovic, the head of the physics department at the College of Liberal Arts, to help me design a study for my thesis on powder magnetism. By then Professor Jovanovic was my father-in-law and I called him Cika Dragi. I did talk to Cika Dragi, and with his assistant Vladimir Skolnik's help, I did a neat study. The title of my thesis was "A study of the magnetic properties of the thermal decomposition products of ferrous oxalate in an atmosphere of carbon dioxide."

Later, Vlada and I happened to be on the same ship to the United States, and we stayed good friends until his death in 1990.

School was in session six days a week. After a long day at his school or at the Nuclear Institute in Vinca, Drasko would wait for me in front of my university building. We walked across the street to a restaurant where I had a subscription to eat. I have no clue where Misa or Dad ate in those days. After I ate, we slowly walked toward my home, stopping at a park on the way to smooch or just talk. We got to my home for some more time together, and by midnight Drasko would go home.

I remember one time I could not understand how orders of magnitude were expressed in powers of ten. So, Drasko and I sat in Dvorski park, King's Palace Park, across the street from the Parliament, and Drasko explained the mathematics of it. And I understood. I guess it was Drasko's knowledge and interest in learning that truly attracted me to him. All my other friends were primarily concerned with how to have more fun. To study was a burden we all had to live with. I actually loved my courses and was happy to find a kindred spirit in Drasko. He was good looking to boot. He had great legs and a cute butt. His only deficiency was his age. He was only a year older than I, and in those days boyfriends were expected to be at least four years older.

++

While I was still in high school my father worked in a wholesale food company. He was in charge of their warehouse and often brought home food and liqueur samples. Living on the main square in town and having access to fine liqueurs, I developed a large circle of friends. In addition, my summer friends from Sombor were now university students in Belgrade.

The first year in college, before Drasko and I started going steady, my social life did not change much. We still went for walks along the promenade and had informal gatherings, mostly in my apartment. Many of my friends played the piano, and we danced. But all that slowly died away due to six days a week of hard work at college and going to the mountains to hike on Sundays.

We would get on a train on Saturday evening, hike a mountain all day Sunday, and come home dead tired Sunday night. More often than not I would break out with cold sores as a result of being totally exhausted. There were several three- or four-day national holidays when we did big hikes. These were Tito's birthday, May 25; Belgrade Liberation Day, October 20; Day of the Republic, November 29; and May Day, May 1. There were no religious holydays during communist rule in Yugoslavia. The Belgrade Mountaineering Council or individual clubs organized the big hikes. On occasions when a large number of hikers signed up to go, a special train was provided that dropped us off close to the foothills and picked us up at the same or another designated place.

Between 1949 and 1956, I hiked Suva planina, Stolovi, Korab, Prokletije, Durmitor, Prenj, Tara, Triglav, Mojstrovka, Prisank, Mangart, and many other mountains across Yugoslavia.

The university was in session from September until May. January and June were exam months. It was each student's decision when to take the exam for the courses he or she was enrolled in. One could take the exam years after taking the course. Good students, of course, took all the exams at the end of the course. If you failed, you could take the same exam the next exam term, or the next or the next. Many were students for years or never got their degrees.

Drasko and I were total nerds. We both got our degrees on time. B.S. in physics was a four-year course, and B.S. in engineering was a five-and-a-half year course plus a thesis (diplomski rad). I started college in September 1949 and graduated in February 1956.

In 1953, as a fourth-year metallurgy student, I spent two summer months in Borski rudnik, one of the world's largest copper mine and copper production plant. I spent time with each phase of the production, from digging the ore to producing pure copper ingots.

At different times during my college years, my whole class visited other metal production plants in the country. After the fifth year, my classmates spent the summer at various metal production plants in other European countries. Because I was of bourgeois background, I was not allowed to go. I was told that I was not able to represent the Socialist Republic and its constitution. The funny thing was that I could not care less. I had a free summer to do what I wanted.

By the summer of 1950, Drasko and I were going steady. We did everything together. Here is a brief description of our summer activities. In 1950, we spent a month in a mountaineering leaders training camp at Plavsko jezero in Montenegro and then a couple of weeks on Bled jezero in Slovenija. In 1951, we camped at Crno jezero on Durmitor for a couple of weeks or more and from there went to Dubrovnik for a week or so. In 1952, we camped at Boracko jezero and then again went to Dubrovnik. The day or multiple-day hikes were done from the camps. In between these trips we spent time in Soko Banja at Drasko's family summer home.

We took trains, local trucks, or horse-drawn wagons to get as close to a campsite as possible. Our provisions were unloaded somewhere along the road and we would backpack them to the campsite in multiple trips. We always camped next to a lake (jezero) that provided water and swimming. We brought food with us or we bought it in nearby villages. I remember at Boracko jezero we had to take wheat grain to the local mill to be ground, and then we took the flour to the village bakery to exchange for bread. We brought the grain with us from home.

In the early fifties university students were receiving food supplies from the UNRA, the United Nations Relief Agency. Five-pound cans of bacon, powdered eggs, and orange marmalade came in very handy as our camping staples.

We also hiked and skied during the winter breaks. But winter sports were never our favorite. Tara, Kopaonik, Kranjska Gora and Jezersko were some of the places we went to in the winter. One memorable winter trip to Kopaonik mountain was a scientific expedition.

Vlasta Vucic, Professor of Physics at the Department of Mechanical Engineering, organized the trip to collect samples of radioactive waters. Vlasta was Drasko's first cousin, Cika Dragi's older sister Zivka's son and father of Julia (Beba) and Arijana (Cuca). Drasko, Mita Sakovic, Mica Milanovic and I went with Vlasta to Kopaonik where we worked and hiked. Mita was also Drasko's first cousin. He was Tetkica Mileva's son, Cika Dragi's younger sister. Mita died of cancer soon after. Mica, a civil engineering student and Drasko's best friend, was later the best man at our wedding. We spent several sunny days in glorious, unspoiled snow covered nature, looking for hot springs, and collecting water samples. Vlasta was measuring concentrations of radon in hot springs. We stayed in the comforts of one of the mountain lodges.

++

I was thirteen when WWII ended. During the war we all learned not to speak against the Germans or against the partisans. If you were reported, you might get shot, hanged, sent to a concentration camp, or your house got burned down. It was not much different under Tito's rule. You kept your mouth shut and lived the best you could. I learned not to say or to write down anything that might haunt me then or years from then. To this day I do the same. Drasko's political arguments over the web forums or the letters he writes to all sorts of authorities, from the President of the United States to the editor of *The New York Times*, give me the creeps. He thinks he is safe in his armchair, but a single knock on our front door by a government agent would give us both heart attacks.

There were three levels of the communist regime that affected my life. In my apartment building there was the local Communist Party cell. On our street there was Narodni Front, the People's Front organization. At the university there was Studentska Omladina, the student youth organization. There was also Skojevci, a communist youth organization. To be a member of Skojevci or the Communist Party, you had to be deserving and dedicated to the cause. Because of my family background, I could never achieve that, nor did I want to.

My home was the only place where I did not have to worry about what I said. You simply did not trust anybody else. I obediently attended all required street organization meetings. Luckily there were not that many of them. It was a different story at the university. There was a period when we had a political meeting every evening from seven until midnight. On those evenings Drasko would wait for me, and we would hold hands and slowly walk to my home. He never got home before two in the morning, and the next morning at six o'clock, he was on the bus to the Nuclear Institute at Vinca.

Several university communist party leaders were in my class. I think it was politically correct for them to become metallurgists and be the ones to build the badly needed heavy industry in the country. When in class I learned not to talk about anything but school. My activities as a member of the Belgrade Mountaineering Council made up for not being politically active at the university. I kept to myself, and at the same time, I was friends with everybody. None of my fellow students were ever in my home, nor was I in theirs. I barely remember any of them.

Branka Jovanovic, my sister-in-law, the widow of Drasko's younger brother Manojlo (Leka), is six years younger than I am. Her life as a student was totally different from mine. All the political pressures or threats to one's freedom were gone from the university life. Only six years after me, she was spared the communist political pressure. This is reflected in her attitude toward Yugoslavia. I never got free from the fear that anything could happen to you when in Yugoslavia. Every time I went back for a visit, the first thing I did was phone the American Embassy to tell them I am in the country. Branka never did that.

In my time individual freedom simply did not exist. It was up to me to protect myself and to create a world within which I was free. Studying and hiking did that for me. I was truly a friend with very few people: Drasko and my family. Sad, but true! Having Drasko, I really did not need anybody else. I suspect my fellow students thought of me as a nerd in love.

I made sure I did all that was expected of me. I attended the meetings. I voted (you got a little rubber ball that you dropped into the only candidate box). I attended endless student youth organization meetings. Altogether, I survived without ever stepping on anybody's political foot.

The lessons I learned stayed with me forever. Throughout my life I am careful not to say, write or sign anything that I might be sorry for later. During the 1950s I read Ayn Rand's *The Fountainhead*, where the protagonist was ruined by the McCarthy investigation because he had signed a petition earlier in his life. I could not believe how stupid he must have been. It took me a long time to realize that in a free country it is okay to stand up for your beliefs.

I also learned how to be friends with people from all walks of life. That served me well when I dealt with people in Washington, DC, with funding agencies, contractors, and various service people from cleaning to sales. I probably don't even know how to make an enemy. Is this good or bad? I do not know and I do not care much.

++

My religious, foreign language and pre-army education reflected the times. Before WWII, the catechism was part of the curriculum in elementary school. We had a thin book that we studied—the Ten Commandments, beatitudes, proverbs, prayers, and stories from the Old and New Testaments. I have never seen a Bible outside of church. It was written in Latin or maybe in an old Slavic church language. I did not even know that common people could own Bibles. I discovered much later that we had a translated Serbian version that Deda Ceda owned, obviously not to be seen or touched by anybody else in the family. It was a small book with a small print, which I now own. My father probably gave it to me when he came to visit in 1962, hoping that I would not be totally lost to my heritage. I do not remember ever having again any formal instruction in religion after 1941.

Throughout the years, we celebrated three main religious holidays at home: Christmas on January 7, Easter, and Slava. Slava was the Patron Saint day on which the family's ancestors were baptized into Christianity. Archangel Michael day on November 21 was the Dimitrijevic family Slava. The priest came to our home to bless Slava day. He cut Slava's specially made and shaped milk bread, burned incense (tamjan) and performed a short service. The priest had an assistant (pojac) who sang along with the priest's chanting.

There were many different Slava days. Friends and family were obliged to visit and wish happy Slava to everyone who celebrated on the same patron saint day. On major saints' days like St. Nicholas, Archangel Michael and St. John, I spent the whole day going from home to home visiting. I actually loved to do that, because the food offered was always great. There was boiled wheat grain ground with equal parts of walnuts and sugar (koljivo), candied fruits (slatko), and a variety of cookies and cakes (tortas). A hundred people or more could go through our home on Slava day. The preparation of food took several days, if not longer.

Christmas was a three-day holiday celebrated on January 7. On Christmas Eve, while the family waited in the hallway, angels brought and decorated a tree in the dining room. When the bell rang, my grandmother, Majka Stanka, led a procession through the house while burning incense (tamjan). The rest of us carried straw that we threw on the floor creating a manger throughout the house. Under the Christmas tree, which was lit with candles, were the presents. The presents were not wrapped and were grouped with a big name tag so you immediately knew what Santa Claus (Bozic Bata) brought for you. I don't remember ever seeing a wrapped gift until I came to the United States. The main activity on Christmas day was the big midday meal, followed by short visits of friends throughout the rest of the day. For us kids the big deal was cesnica, a form of baklava without nuts that was served at the end of the meal and in which a gold coin was hidden. Whoever got the piece with the coin sold it back to Deda Ceda and received real money for it. Of course, one of us children always found the coin.

The only time I had to go to church was on Great Thursday before Easter. This was a several hour long, complicated midnight service that I did not like to attend. Eastern Orthodox Churches had no seats and standing for hours was hard. I know I went to church before WWII more often. During the war, and especially under the communist regime, I did not go to church. I never truly learned what church was all about. The little bit I learned in elementary school did not tell me much. Everything related to church was done in an old Slavic language nobody understood. You became Eastern Orthodox at birth, and that was it. I did not even know that there were other major religions until I came to the United States. In my world, our Eastern Orthodox religion (pravoslavna vera) was the most important one, and Roman Catholicism, the wrong one. I had no clue that Jews represented another religion. Small Protestant groups existed, but I never connected them to a church.

Tito's communist regime separated the church from the state. To be an active member of the church was not desirable, if not outright antigovernment. Thus, church disappeared out of my life. I was happy not to have to go to church anymore, and because lightning did not strike, I was okay. One consequence of this was that Drasko and I never got married in the church. But thanks to Teta Mira, Drasko's mom, and Irena, my brother's wife, and Jasna, when we visited in 1981, Misa's children, Ivan and Marko, and my children, Jasna and Vesna, were baptized in Saborna Church in Belgrade. I was the godmother to Misa's children, and Misa was the godfather to mine.

At the other end of my education spectrum was my pre-army education, predvojnicka obuka. It was a full-credit course I had to take both in high school and at the university. We were instructed in offensive and defensive tactics, arms, and who knows what else. An army officer taught the course. I participated in one of the maneuvers, where hundreds of students spent the day in the fields outside of Belgrade conducting an imaginary war. I carried a rifle all day, and we moved from place to place. That is all I remember.

Somewhere in the middle was my foreign language education. It strictly reflected the times. Before WWII, I had a German-speaking governess and private French lessons. During the war we had German in school. After the war Russian was obligatory in high school. I also had English as an elective. At the university I had English as my foreign language elective course. Of all these languages, I learned enough English to be able to study from English textbooks and to read my collection of paperbacks. I knew German and Russian equally well, enough to communicate if necessary, but not enough to read. I hardly learned any French at all. After I came to the United States, it took me three months to become reasonably fluent in spoken English. The other languages are long forgotten.

++

During our college years we befriended a group of physics students from Drasko's department. Bogoljub (Boza) Lalevic, Jovan (Joca) Jovanovic, Miroslav (Tosa) Todorovic, Nikola (Nidja) Nikolic and Vladimir (Vlada) Skolnik were excellent students. Drasko gravitated to them even though they were a couple of classes ahead of him. I liked their wives, Marija Lalevic, Anica Jovanovic, and Branka Todorovic, very much.

Tosa was the one who triggered their going to the United States by becoming the first graduate student in the group. He wrote to a Columbia University professor, author of a textbook Tosa was using, asking him about the graduate program in physics education. The letter Tosa received in response convinced the authorities at the Nuclear Institute at Vinca that it would be important for Tosa to go to Columbia and learn new physics. With the help of Branka's uncle, an academic from Zagreb and his long-time friend at Westinghouse Corporation in the United States, Tosa became a graduate student at Columbia University. This was not a small feat since in those days Universities in the United States were not accepting students from communist countries. In February 1954,

Tosa left for America.

Soon after, Tosa helped Nidja become a graduate student at Columbia. Joca was accepted at the University of Winnipeg, Canada. Later, Joca helped Vlada to get there too. Drasko and Boza were selected to receive stipends provided by the American Technical Assistance for the Undeveloped Nations through the Yugoslav Atomic Energy Commission. The main reason they were selected was that in addition to being among the best young physicists, they were not members of the Communist Party, one of the fellowships' conditions. So in September 1954, Boza went to Princeton and Drasko to the University of Chicago. The four wives, Marija, Branka, Anica and I, were left behind.

In July 1954, I went with Drasko to the American Embassy to get his visa. The consul asked who I was. We explained, and he promptly suggested we get married before Drasko left for the United States. We thought Drasko was going for a year of specialization. The consul explained that Drasko was going to be a graduate student and might be in the United States for several years. If I planned to visit him, we would have to be married. So, we decided to get married in a hurry. It was midsummer and our families were out of town. The Jovanovics were in Soko Banja and could not come back on short notice. I do not remember where my dad and my stepmother Katica were, but they did come home in time to organize a wedding reception for us.

So, on August 8, 1954, Drasko and I, and our witnesses, Mica Milanovic and Mira Danicic, went to our Terazije District City Hall. We stood in line for a couple of hours with other couples and got married. I remember it happened in a big room with two people standing behind a desk. I do not recall what was said. We signed a big book and that was it. Then the four of us went next door to a photographer for our wedding pictures. I had on a mustard yellow two-piece dress.

At home, Dad and Katica had prepared a feast. Many people came to congratulate us, but I have no recollection of who came. I remember Cika Zarko playing the wedding march on the piano. Dad gave us our wedding rings, and we put them on. Drasko and I had obtained the rings a few days earlier in Mihajlo Petkovic's jewelry store in my building, in exchange for a gold coin my family had.

After the wedding and until September, when Drasko left for the United States, we lived for a few days in my home and a few days in Drasko's. If Drasko's departure had not been imminent, we would not have married for a few more years. The main reason was the lack of living space. Apartments for rent did not exist. After WWII, a large influx of people from the rural areas came looking for work. The destruction due to the bombing and the lack of new construction made housing very scarce. The government owned all of the real estate and distributed apartments to its own deserving people, mostly partisan heroes and high-ranking government functionaries.

Families like mine rented part of their homes to students and others who worked in Belgrade, but who had no place to live. At different times during those years, four students from out of town and one journalist lived in our third room. All of them became our friends, including Irena who later married my brother, Misa. Drasko and I were hoping that, once we have graduated, one of our respective future job institutions would provide us with housing. Until then, like everybody else, we were planning to go steady.

As soon as Drasko settled in at the University of Chicago, he wrote to tell me that it would take five years to get a Ph.D. in physics, and that he was going to do it. Therefore, I had to find a way to join him. I promptly went to the American Embassy to ask the consul how to obtain a visa. He told me that the only way I could get to the United States was also as a student. Drasko was not in a position to support a wife, and the consul would not give me a tourist visa because I would want to stay as long as Drasko was there. Thus, I embarked on a long and complicated process of trying to figure out where and how to become a student for the sake of the visa and to find a way to convince the Yugoslav authorities to give me a passport.

In the long run, it was easier to get the visa than to get the passport. The two activities were not connected. I wrote to Vera Laska, the foreign student admission officer at the University of Chicago, and a friend of Drasko's, who explained to me that without a car, there was no way I could physically live with Drasko and attend any school other then the University of Chicago. She mailed me the application forms that I filled out with the help of two friends. Robert Kragalott was an American Fulbright Fellow and Dragan Popovic was Drasko's colleague from Vinca, who had spent some time abroad. Dragan suggested that I study uranium chemistry, because the University of Chicago was famous in that field. My professors were more than happy to write the recommendations. This must have happened in the fall of 1955. In April 1956, I was accepted at the University of Chicago with a tuition waiver and a promise of a student technician job to support myself. In the meantime, Vera Laska and her husband, Andy, wrote an affidavit of support for me, so there was no delay in getting the visa. I received the passport through Vinca as Drasko's wife going for a short visit that was valid only until May 1956. It was imperative that I get a visa quickly and leave the country. The consul understood that and was very accommodating.

Once I was accepted at the University of Chicago, Dragan Popovic suggested I talk to Pavle Savic, director of the Nuclear Institute at Vinca, and request that Vinca pay my trip to the United States. In return, I would work at Vinca, once I learned uranium chemistry. I went to the chemistry department where Pavle Savic was also a professor, knocked on the door, and got through several doors to Pavle Savic's office. I suspect that being Dragoljub Jovanovic's daughter-in-law helped in opening those doors. Cika Dragi made it possible for Pavle Savic, as his assistant in earlier days, to work in the Curie Institute in Paris, France. This may have been a payback from which I benefited. Pavle Savic agreed to have Vinca make a contract with me and pay for my trip. Originally, Cika Bora, my stepfather, gave me his life savings to buy the ticket to the United States on board of one of the Yugoslav merchant marine ships. To give him back his money was a great relief all around. Travel costs to foreign countries in those days were totally beyond anybody's financial means.

Based on a letter from the Nuclear Institute at Vinca that gave me permission to visit Drasko, who was considered to be in the United States on official Vinca business, I applied for a passport. This was in the days when only deserving communist types were getting to travel abroad. Once my application was in, I was invited for an interview, where a passport official tried to convince me that Drasko probably had already found a new girlfriend and I should not bother to go. When I did not respond to that, he told me that the leader of the Communist Party cell in my apartment building, who happened to be our janitor, stated that I did not deserve to get a passport since I was of bourgeois background. In the end I did get a passport for a limited time period to visit Drasko who was still officially in the United States for one year to specialize in physics.

The good thing was that different parties tried their best to help me get to the United States. The big problem would have been if I had not been able to leave the country that May 1956 and had had to apply for a new passport. I would have never obtained it, because Drasko refused to come back after the fellowship expired and stayed in the United States to complete his graduate degree. Neither Vinca nor the Atomic Energy Commission cared less what Drasko wanted to do. They abandoned him to his own fate in the United States. As his wife, I would not have been able to get a new permission letter from Vinca to visit Drasko or to apply for a passport again. I did leave Yugoslavia on April 25, 1956 in the nick of time. My passport was due to expire on May 11, 1956, the day I arrived in the United States.

After Drasko left for the United States, Marija, Anica, Branka and I did our best to keep our morale high. The three of them were older than me and were already done with college. Marija was a chemist in Vinca, Anica a medical doctor, and Branka a pianist. Marija was the first to leave for the United States. She left a few weeks before I did. Then I left, and then Branka in November and Anica in

December 1956. We all stayed good friends and provided moral support to each other while finding our way in the United States. Over the years we had many reunions: in St. Louis, Minneapolis, New York, Chicago, Long Island, Cape May Point, Driggs, Cape Cod, on a lake in Minnesota, and Winnipeg. This year, June 2003, we are getting together in Cape May Point again for Marija and Boza's 50th wedding anniversary. After forty-eight years we are much older but still peppy. It will be a happy event. The only sad thing is that Vlada Skolnik will not be there.

++

Milica (Mima) Gavanski was another good friend who helped me survive the lonely days after Drasko left. She and I started chemical engineering together, and while I became a metallurgist, she was graduated as a chemical engineer. She was a beautiful blond, very smart, and very popular. She came from a pre-WWII wealthy family and knew everybody in town. I was adopted by her group and as a result had a very nice social life during the time I was alone. Her friends became my friends. Jasna Jovanovic, who later married Bob Kragalott and moved to the United States, was a curator in the Nikola Tesla Museum in Belgrade. She became a university professor of linguistics in Columbus, Ohio. Ljubica Popovic, an art historian, also came to the United States and was a professor of art history at Vanderbilt University. Only Mima stayed behind. We tried to get her to come visit us, but she never wanted to. For her, life in Belgrade was the greatest, and the United States was the boonies. I do have very pleasant memories of my friendship with Mima.

++

I spent the summer of 1955 vacationing with Coka. We spent a month in Log pod Mangartom in Slovenija. We hiked a lot and generally had a good time. Then we went to Opatija, a major resort on the Adriatic, for a week or two. I remember sitting with Coka in a garden restaurant on the beach and discussing my future. Coka was very proud of my achievements and fully supported my going to America to join Drasko. Most people, including me, knew very little about that country. We knew all about the Mafia, the gangsters, and the Wild West, and little else. Information about life in the United States was scarce. What we saw in the movies, read in available literature, and learned through hearsay was not very encouraging. We believed America was far from being civilized. But I figured if Drasko was happy there, I would be happy too. Thanks to Mima's social connection at the American Embassy, I did listen to Frank Sinatra, Doris Day, Dinah Shore and Bing Crosby records. This was jazz to me, and I loved it, a very favorable attribute of the United States.

It was hard to say goodbye to my family and friends. Misa graduated from law school in January 1956, and we had said goodbye in March when he left to serve in the army. The day before I left home, I received a goodbye postcard from Coka, who could not come to Belgrade, because school was in session. The day before I left, I stopped by to visit and receive hugs and kisses from my mom and Cika Bora. I also stopped by to say goodbye to Drasko's parents. Other friends and relatives came to Terazije to say goodbye. I parted with Anica and Branka with a heavy heart, because it was not clear that they would make it to the United States. My dad was the only one who came with me to Rijeka, the port on the Adriatic Sea, and saw the ship *Hrvatska* depart. But, even though it was hard to leave home, I was totally excited and could not wait to see Drasko again after twenty months of separation. A new world and a new life was waiting for me, and I was looking forward to it.

EPILOGUE

Reading over what I wrote, I realized that I never questioned why my parents were divorced or why Misa and I lived with my father and not with my mother. I never questioned why my mom never came to visit us at home. On her regular visits to Zemun, Misa and I would wait to see her from the window and then run downstairs to meet her. She often came with her sister Marija whom we called Tetka Beba. We spent time in parks, the bakery and other places but not in our home. During WWII we saw her very little, if at all. After the war, when she moved to Belgrade, we became great friends, with no restrictions on visits of any kind. It could be that while Deda Ceda was alive, different rules applied. I never detected any animosity or dislike between my mom and dad once she started to visit us at home. I also liked my stepfather, Cika Bora, very much. He was a gentle, sophisticated man, and always happy to see me.

The only explanation is that Misa and I were totally happy with our lives. My dad, Majka Stanka, and Coka, our core family adored us. Deda Ceda did too, but he was too busy and did not spend much time with us. We had a large extended family that loved us, and our lives were happy and fun. In retrospect, I do wonder why no one ever said a word about my parents' situation. Literally, no one ever brought the subject up. Deda Ceda was the only one who carried the "as-their-mother-left-them" photo of Misa and me. Misa and I and the rest of the family thought that was funny. Was it? I don't know.

DIMITRIJEVIC FAMILY TREE
2008

Cedomilj (Ceda) Dimitrijevic
1866 – 1944
& Konstancija (Stanka) Stojanovic
1872 – 1954

Vukica Dimitrijevic
1895 – 1903

Milos Dimitrijevic
1896 – 1975
& Emilija (Mila) Tabakovic
1906 – 1981

Milos Dimitrijevic
1896 – 1975
& Katalina (Katica) Vasiljevic
1896 – 1990

Zorka-Beba Dimitrijevic
1899 – 1991
& Lazar (Laza) Ilijevic
1889 – 1979

Zagorka (Cicika) Dimitrijevic
1902 – 1985
& Sveta Jeftic

Zagorka (Cicika) Dimitrijevic
1902 – 1985
& Svetozar Murgaski
1903 – 1979

Milica Dimitrijevic
1903 – 1956
& Jeno (Gena) Hajto
1897 – 1990

Sofija (Coka) Dimitrijevic
1905 – 1992

Mihajlo Dimitrijevic
1906 – 1979
& Maca Lazic

Mihajlo Dimitrijevic
1906 – 1979
& Eta Kovacs
1921 – 2006

Zarko Dimitrijevic
1908 – 1995
& Gordana Osmec
1912 – ?

Zarko Dimitrijevic
1908 – 1995
& Mara Markovic
1921 – 2001

Stanka Dimitrijevic
1931
& Drasko Jovanovic
1930

Mihailo (Misa) Dimitrijevic
1032
& Jasminka Jovicic
1933

Mihailo (Misa) Dimitrijevic
1932
& Irena Sipos
1943 – 2008

Ksenija Ilijevic
1923 – 2005

Marica Jeftic
1923 – 1936

Aurel Hajto
1929 – 2001
& Jutka Kolba
1937

Benjamin (Beba) Hajto
1930
& Olga Takacs
1942

Jeno (Ocsi) Hajto
1938
& Ildiko Kezdi-Kovacs
1942

Sofia (Zsofia) Hajto
1940 – 2005
& Miklos Beladi
1928 – 1983

Cedomir (Ceda) Dimitrijevic
1953
& Vukica Beljanski
1953

Zlatibor (Bata) Dimitrijevic
1954
& Vera Grujic
1947

Jasna Diane Jovanovic
1963
& Thomas James Mackin
1957

Vesna Ann Jovanovic
1967

Ivan Dimitrijevic
1974

Marko Dimitrijevic
1976

Gabor Hajto
1963

Laszlo Hajto
1965

Zoltan Hajto
1967
& Ildiko Farkas
1970

Gyula Hajto
1989

Jan Hajto
1968
& Daniela Fric
1968

Natali Hajto
1969
& Tamas Gyongyossi
1953

Andras (Marci) Beladi
1971
& Frida Farkas
1974

Ivana Dimitrijevic
1979

Martina Dimitrijevic
1988

Dorotea Dimitrijevic
1990

Sasa Dimitrijevic
1979

Mihajlo Dimitrijevic
1980

Matejas Walter
Jovanovic Mackin
1998

Lukas Milos
Jovanovic Mackin
2000

Oscar Dimitri
Jovanovic
2008

Balazs Peter Hajto
2001

Kristof Andras Hajto
2002

Marcell Tamas Hajto
2006

Julius Hajto
2001

Sophia Hajto
2003

Mark Gyongyossi
1995

Kyra Gyongyossi
1996

Fanni Beladi
2001

Kamilla Beladi
2003

Andras Beladi
2005

Marko Dimitrijevic
2008

Natasa Dimitrijevic
2004

Nevena Dimitrijevic
2006

MAP OF YUGOSLAVIA
Places mentioned in text are indicated.

▲ **Mountains and Lakes (jezero)**

1. Juliske Alpe (Julian Alps): Triglav Mojstrovka Prisank Mangart
2. Prenj
3. Boracko jezero
4. Durmitor
5. Tara
6. Prokletije
7. Plavsko jezero
8. Avala
9. Stolovi
10. Kopaonik
11. Ljuboten
12. Korab
13. Suva planina

● **Towns**

1. Log pod Mangartom
2. Kranjska Gora Mojstrana Gozd Martuljek
3. Bled
4. Opatija
5. Rijeka
6. Split
7. Dubrovnik
8. Sarajevo
9. Sombor
10. Subotica
11. Zmajevo (Pasicevo)
12. Temerin
13. Novi Sad
14. Sremski Karlovci
15. Kikinda
16. Zrenjanin (Beckerek)
17. Zemun
18. Pancevo
19. Belgrade
20. Vinca
21. Arandjelovac Banja
22. Smederevska Palanka
23. Borski rudnik
24. Soko Banja

A NOTE ON NAMES AND PRONOUNCIATIONS

Definitions
<u>Serbian — English</u>
Baba* — Grandmother
Baka* — Grandmother
Cika (Čika) — Uncle, my parents brothers and cousins
Deda — Grandfather
Majka* — Grandmother
Strina — Wives of fathers' brothers
Teca (Teča) — Aunt's husbands
Tetka — Aunts, my parents sisters and cousins
*Which word was used to address a grandmother depended on the family.
The meaning of the words is the same

Serbian Spelling and Pronunciation
(ž = zh (Zhivago); č = hard ch; ć = soft ch; š = sh

<u>People</u>
Boza — Boža
Bozic Bata — Božic Bata
Ceda — Čeda
Cedomir — Čedomir
Cenejac — Čenejac
Danicic — Daničić
Dimitrijevic — Dimitrijević
(same for all last names ending in "ic")
Drasko — Draško
Mica — Mića
Milos — Miloš
Misa — Miša
Miska — Miška
Skolnik — Školnik
Stancika — Štancika
Tosa — Toša
Vucic — Vučić
Zarko — Žarko
Zivka — Živka
Ziskovic — Žišković

<u>Places</u>
Backa — Bačka
Beckerek — Bečkerek
Becej — Bečej
Pancevo — Pančevo
Tamis — Tamiš
Bezaniska kosa — Bežaniska kosa
Pasicevo — Pašićevo
Pacir — Pačir
Radnicki — Radnički
Kolarcev universitet — Kolarčev universitet
Vracar — Vračar
Boracko jezero — Boračko jezero
Vinca — Vinča

BOOK II

MY LIFE IN AMERICA

1956–2004

STANKA JOVANOVIC

INTRODUCTION

After I had finished writing *My Life in Yugoslavia* I realized that my life in America was equally unusual, and that my children might like to know more about it. I arrived in the United States of America in 1956 with one suitcase and ninety dollars in my pocket, a far cry from what Drasko, my husband, and I have today. Our dedicated effort to finish graduate school, to do as good a job as we could in our respective professions, to build a rich family life, and to be good people brought us to the happy life we have today.

I started writing this book last summer, 2003, in our house in Driggs, Idaho. I finished writing it in March 2004 during our winter stay in our condo on Hutchinson Island in Florida. Then it took me two months to go through the hundreds of wonderful slides and photos we have to arrive at the set of fifty-five pictures you will see here. To select 'meaningful' photos was a much more complicated process than I expected it to be. I had to remind myself that the emphasis of this book is on my life and not on my family's life. Of course, one could not separate one from the other, but I did try to keep the focus on me.

To tell a coherent story I extracted from the main body of the text my education and my professional life as a separate chapter. I also added a brief chapter, just an overview, on Drasko's, and my daughters', Jasna and Vesna, lives.

There are also several appendices. A list of my professional publications as a research chemist is appended primarily so that it is preserved for posterity. My Fermilab-related curriculum vitae and an article from the Chicago Tribune give an overview of my activities during my tenure as the Fermilab Education Office Manager.

A Jovanovic family tree is appended as a bonus. My Dimitrijevic family tree, my father's family, was included in *My Life in Yugoslavia*.

I reused it here as part of the 1988 Dimitrijevic Family Reunion story. I have also appended 'A Note on Names and Pronunciation' of Serbian words, a simpler version of the one that appeared in *My Life in Yugoslavia.*

I am seventy-three years old this year. If I live another ten years, I may write one more sequel to my life. Let's wait and see.

July, 2004

PROLOGUE

When I arrived in America in 1956 I thought of myself as a well-educated person. I had a university degree, I was well-read and I grew up in a family of educated people. But coming to the United States of America was like making a cultural leap in time. Due to WWII and the Cold War, the Western world had left us in Eastern Europe behind in every possible way: in science and technology, in economic development, in democracy and in individual freedom.

I had a lot of catching up to do. I had to upgrade my educational background so that I could follow the graduate courses I was taking at the University of Chicago. Even though I could read English, I had to learn how to speak and understand the spoken word. I had to learn how to shop and what to buy. The way food was packaged and sold was totally new to me. At home you would go to a butcher who would cut a chunk of meat for you from a hanging carcass. You would go to an open market to buy fruits and vegetables. You would go to a grocery store to buy staples, like flour and sugar. You would go to a dairy, to a baker, etc. Then I had to learn how to determine my size in everything. Here, all clothing was ready-made and easily available. Nothing was made by a seamstress, or a tailor, or by an aunt. We had no television, no access to cars and no bank accounts. All that, and much more, was new to me.

But, I was a quick learner and it was easy to adjust to a much richer life than I had back home. Many good people befriended me and were happy to answer my questions and provide guidance. When I arrived in Chicago Drasko, my husband, was in his third year of graduate school and was still learning, too. Together, and within a short time, we became Americanized, and ever since our lives have been productive, fruitful, and great fun.

TRIP TO AMERICA AND LIFE IN CHICAGO
1956–1960

I left Yugoslavia on my twenty-fifth birthday, April 25, 1956, from Rijeka, a major port on the Adriatic Sea. My father, Milos Dimitrijevic, was at the shore waving good-bye as my ship left the port. I was very sad and very happy at the same time. I was on my way to Drasko, my husband, to the University of Chicago graduate school and to a new life I could not even imagine. My heavy leather suitcase and I shared a cabin with an older lady who was on her way to America to join her son and his family. There were sixteen passengers on the Yugoslav cargo ship *Hrvatska*. My friend Vlada Skolnik was on board on his way to graduate school at the University of Manitoba in Winnipeg, Canada. I also remember Bosko Djordjevic who was on his way to graduate school at Rutgers University in New Jersey. I do not remember anybody else.

The passengers' cabins and the dining room were all on one deck. The rest of the ship was off limits to the passengers. The crew was busy everywhere and we would have been in the way. We must have been on the second or third deck with nice views of the blue Adriatic Sea, the Mediterranean and then the Atlantic Ocean. The food was excellent and much better than I had at home. In addition to great meals and desserts there was freshly baked bread for every meal. The seas were calm and friendly, other than one stormy night we weathered strapped to our beds.

The captain and the officers commingled with the passengers. The First Officer cast his eyes on me, but quickly found out I was not interested in a shipboard affair. We became good friends and had fun all the way to New York. The ship docked in Tangier, Morocco for a day. The First Officer and I went sightseeing, including visiting the bazaar. It was quite a culture shock to see all the goods displayed all over the stores and the streets. The First Officer insisted on buying me a birthday present. After serious deliberation I decided that what I really wanted was a pair of translucent nylon panties. I had never seen anything like those before. He happily bought a pair for me. Later, back on the ship, I proudly showed my gift with no thought of how appropriate, or inappropriate it was. I was happy and that was most important to me.

The only other place we came close to any land was in passing through the Scylla and Charybdis channel between Sicily and Italy. On the way out from Tangier we passed close to the Rock of Gibraltar. Once on the open ocean we saw no land until we sighted the Statue of Liberty. An emotional testimony that I was in America and soon to be with Drasko.

+++

In the morning on May 11, 1956 we docked in Brooklyn. After clearing with the immigration authorities that came aboard the ship, I disembarked to find Marija and Bogoljub (Boza) Lalevic, Nikola (Nidja) Nikolic and Miroslav (Tosa) Todorovic waiting for Vlada Skolnik and me. We were all good friends from back home. The men were all physicists and good friends who had helped each other get to graduate school in the United States and Canada. Missing were Jovan (Joca) Jovanovic, who was already in Canada, and Branka Todorovic and Anica Jovanovic. They were still in Yugoslavia waiting for their visas and passports to be able to join their husbands.

From the port we all went to Tosa's aunt's house in Brooklyn where I was to stay for a week while waiting for Drasko to finish taking his "basic" exam at the University of Chicago. I did not want to disturb him while he was studying, and then taking this very important exam. Passing the exam would allow him to continue his studies toward a Ph. D. degree. Later that afternoon the Lalevics left for Princeton, New Jersey, where Boza was a graduate student. Nidja left for his home in Manhattan, where he and Tosa were graduate students at Columbia University.

Once alone with Tosa and his aunt I opened my suitcase and was assailed with the smell of plum brandy (sljivovica). I had brought a bottle with me as a gift to Drasko's and my friends Vera and Andrew (Andy) J. Laska in Chicago. The bottle broke in transport and all my stuff was soaked and smelly. What did we do? We strung clotheslines throughout the living room and hung all to air for the several days I stayed with them.

++

On my first day in the United States Tosa and I took the subway from Brooklyn to Manhattan. We got out somewhere in the vicinity of the Metropolitan Museum. Tosa explained to me how to get the subway back home and left me on my own. I must have had a good map because I do not remember having any problem navigating around town.

My first stop was at the Yugoslav Consulate on 5th Avenue across from the Metropolitan Museum. My passport was expiring in six months. Consequently, the student visa I had as I entered the United States was valid only for a few days. In those days the passport had to be valid for six months longer than the visa. Luckily, both the American Consul in Belgrade and the immigration officers on board the ship understood the reasons why my passport had such a short life. It was much easier to extend the passport at a Yugoslav Consulate in the United States than in the Passport Offices in Belgrade. Thus the first thing I did when I got to New York was to extend my passport. To my surprise a pleasant person in the Yugoslav Consulate actually smiled and extended my passport without any problem. It was an enormous difference from what I was used to in dealing with the authorities at home in socialist Yugoslavia.

From the Consulate I walked straight to the New York Immigration Office located close to where Lincoln Center is today. There another pleasant person explained to me that only the Chicago office could extend my student visa because I would be a student in Illinois and not in New York State. That meant that I would have to get to Chicago sooner then I had planned.

Later that day I telephoned Vera Laska. She was the Foreign Student Admission Officer at the University of Chicago with whom I became friends through correspondence. Vera told me to get on the train on a certain day and she would wait for me at the 63rd Street Illinois Central "IC" Railroad station in Chicago. We were not going to tell Drasko I was coming sooner than planned so he could take his exams in peace. I took all this in stride and eventually arrived and met Vera Laska as planned.

In the meantime I continued my sightseeing in Manhattan. Walking from the Consulate to the Immigration Office I had a good view of the south end of Central Park. To my great surprise there were couples everywhere sitting or lying on the grass smooching to their hearts' content. Not to mention that it was the middle of the day. Back home Drasko and I would stand in line waiting for others to leave a park bench so that we could sit and smooch. Smooching in the daytime or sitting on the grass in the parks was unheard of.

I am not sure what else I did that first day, but while I was in New York I went to the Metropolitan Museum, to the United Nations and to Battery Park. I must have also ogled the stores on 5th Avenue. I am sure I walked and used the subway. I had no money to do it any other way.

++

I did one more thing while in New York. I went to New Haven, Connecticut to visit my Aunt Gordana, the wife of my Uncle Zarko, my father's youngest brother. She had left Yugoslavia in 1951 to visit her parents in Trieste, Italy and never came back to Yugoslavia. Instead she joined her sister Djurdja in New Haven. Djurdja had married an American officer while in Trieste. In civilian life he was a professor at Yale. My uncle Zarko asked me to find out whether she planned to come back home. To me she was obviously settled in New Haven and had no intention of going back. Eventually they did get divorced, and later both remarried.

Several things amazed me while visiting Gordana. She lived in her sister's household that was full of archaeological artifacts. In addition one room was dedicated to mannequins dressed in Serbian folk clothes. I found it ridiculous to have old things displayed in the house. I just did not know any better then. They served me potato chips, which I had never seen before. Again, why anybody would serve fried potatoes to guests was beyond me.

Other than that I had a great visit. George Lam, Gordana's friend whom she later married, was a professor in the Department of Metallurgy at Yale. He took me to see his laboratory. I was fresh out of school with an engineering degree in metallurgy and I was properly impressed with his facility. Then they took me to Yale Commons where portraits of several of Djurdja's husband's ancestors were hanging on the walls. I did not understand the significance of that and probably did not act impressed enough.

I saw Gordana and George Lam once again in 1958. We met in the Russian Tea Room in Manhattan. We stayed in touch via Christmas cards for many years and then one day she asked that we stop communicating. I think that by that time her husband had died and she had lost interest in her old family. I never pursued it.

++

I came to the United States with ninety dollars in my pocket, a gift from my stepfather Borislav (Bora) Mihajlovic. As far as I was concerned I was rich. I have no recollection of the price of the train ticket to Chicago or who paid for it. Maybe in those days travel was much cheaper and I had enough money to buy the ticket myself.

Tosa must have orchestrated my departure from New York because I have no recollection of where and when I got on the train. Nor do I remember anything about the trip. Maybe I traveled at night. Once I was safely in the hands of Vera Laska, life became simple. She knew exactly what I had to do to extend my student visa. She took me to see Jack R. Kerridge, the Foreign Student Advisor, whose office was at the University of Chicago International House. This friendly gentleman issued a new I-20 Form I needed to get my student visa. The next morning Vera Laska took me to the 55th Street IC train station where I caught a train to downtown Chicago.

Again, I must have had a good map because I had no problem finding the Immigration Office. There, another pleasant man issued a new student visa and wished me luck.

While Drasko was still taking his exams believing that I was in New York, Vera and Andy Laska took me to Lake Geneva, Wisconsin. There they played golf all day. Again I was amazed. There were these two smart people hitting a small hard ball with sticks and then chasing it all over the place. I did have the presence of mind not to comment, and I did enjoy the day in the country.

The other memorable event was my very first American meal in Vera's house. They prepared a medium rare steak, a baked potato and an avocado salad for me. I could not eat any of it. They had to refry the steak to well done and had to mash the potato with milk and butter. Avocado I just could not swallow. The Laskas were used to foreign students from all over the world, and took my reactions in stride.

Finally Drasko was done with the exam. Vera called his Dean and found out that Drasko passed the exam. What a relief! Vera also called Drasko who promptly came over, and the twenty months of separation were over.

+++

Vera Laska found us a furnished apartment to sublet for the summer. In the fall we moved into a studio apartment on the corner of University Avenue and 56th Street. It was kitty corner from the northeast corner of the University of Chicago Stagg Field, the football field in whose squash court the first nuclear chain reaction occurred. The Institute for the Study of Metals building where I worked as a student was on the west side, and the Chemistry Department, where I attended classes, was on the south side of Stagg Field. In the late fifties I watched from my lab window as the squash court building was demolished by a crane swinging a big iron ball. A peculiar end to a famous historical site. A year or so later a Henry Moore sculpture marked the site.

Between Drasko and me, we made one hundred and ninety dollars per month. It was just enough for the rent and food. Bubble bath, boiled ham and bananas were the luxuries I could afford and I was happy. We walked everywhere, and everything we needed was close by.

Soon we bought used bicycles, making it easy for us to get to Lake Michigan beaches. Swimming was a very important activity for us. Our favorite beach was The Point at the east end of 55th Street. We swam off the big concrete blocks that lined the beach. The lake was clean and the weather warm. During that summer in 1956, I felt I was on a perpetual vacation.

++

During the Second World War Vera Laska had escaped from Czechoslovakia to Yugoslavia where she was treated well by the local people. She later ended up in a German concentration camp and survived. Somehow after the war was over, Vera got to the United States. There she met and married Andy Laska, also a Czech.

So, when in 1954 Drasko showed up at the University of Chicago as the first graduate student from Yugoslavia, Vera went out of her way to be of help to him. Later Vera and Andy helped me even more. On their own initiative they provided an affidavit of support for me that greatly helped me to get a visa and leave Yugoslavia without delay.

Andy was a businessman. He worked in the International Division of Kendall Company. Later he and Vera spent four years in Puerto Rico and then several years in Sao Paulo, Brazil, where Andy was building factories for Kendall Company. Later they settled in Weston, Massachusetts. Vera became a professor of history at Weston College, while Andy continued with Kendall Company. I believe he eventually became the Head of their International Division. Andy recently passed away. Vera still lives in Weston.

No one could have had better friends then Vera and Andy. Drasko and I were truly lucky to have them in our lives.

++

By the time I arrived in Chicago, Drasko had a network of good friends who became my friends too. The men were all graduate students in physics. Drasko's fellow graduate students under Professor Valentine Telegdi were Hans Sens from Holland; Robert Swanson and his wife Jamie, also physicists; and Richard Lundy, who later married Elizabeth, a student in the Graduate Library School. Then there were Paul Murphy from England and his wife Estie, a physical education teacher at the University of Chicago Lab School; Jerome and Gina Friedman, who lived on the second floor above our first floor studio apartment; and Hans and Mariette Kobrak. Mariette was a graduate student in economics.

Most of these people are still our good friends today. By now they are all retired. Hans Sens married Graca and they had three children. In 1996, two years into his retirement, they divorced. Hans was a professor at Utrecht, Holland, stationed at CERN, European Center for Nuclear Research, in Geneva, Switzerland. He now lives in Nice, France with his friend Odile. We see Hans every few years.

Bob Swanson was a professor at University of California San Diego. We are still in touch with Bob via email, but we have not seen them for many years. Bob and Jamie live in La Jolla, California.

Drasko and Dick Lundy had parallel careers. They were both at Argonne National Laboratory for many years, and then at Fermi National Accelerator Laboratory until they retired. Dick retired early, and in 1989 he and Liz left Illinois and moved to White Salmon, Washington. There, on their own they completely restored an old Victorian house that sits on a cliff above the Columbia River in the Columbia Gorge. Their magnificent view encompasses the Columbia River, the town of Hood River and Mt. Hood in its full glory. We stayed in close touch over the years. Now, ever since Vesna, our younger daughter, lives in Portland, Oregon, we see them often.

Paul and Estie Murphy divorced later in life and Paul remarried. Paul was a professor at the University of Manchester in Manchester, England. Estie is still our close and dear friend. She still lives in Manchester. We see her every two or three years here in the United States.

Elaine Garvin died rather young. Ed remarried and we lost touch. Ed was a physicist at SLAC, Stanford Linear Accelerator

Center, in California. Jerry and Gina also divorced, and he is now married to Tanya. Jerry was a professor at the Massachusetts Institute of Technology. They live in Boston. We saw Jerry often while we were still at Fermilab. Hans Kobrak was a professor at the University of California San Diego, but spent much time doing experiments at Fermilab. The Kobraks still live in San Diego.

Eventually most of us had children and grandchildren. Drasko and I met them all at one time or another. They were all very nice young people, but the only lasting friendships among the next generation developed between the Lundy's and our children.

Back to 1956 and our student years. When we were not busy attending classes, or working, or studying, we did many things together with some or all of our friends. We went to the beach, we bicycled along Lake Michigan shores, we went to the movies and we organized parties and cooked dinners. All of us had one main goal in mind: to graduate as soon as possible and begin real life. And we all achieved that goal successfully. In addition, Dick Lundy received the 1989 National Medal of Technology, and Jerry Friedman received the 1990 Nobel Prize in Physics.

++

Valentine (Val) Telegdi, Drasko's professor, and his wife Lia became our good friends. The first time Val met me he told me that I had to buy a new bra and that I had to shave my legs. I do not think I actually owned a bra until Val told me to go and buy one. And I did. Shaving my legs was an unknown concept to me. I did ask around and found out that indeed women in the United States shave their legs and underarms. So I did, too, but I was not very happy about it.

The fact that I had never learned how to cook came back to haunt me. The Telegdis were our very first dinner guests. I served a baked chicken and a package of white sandwich bread as the main course, and a bar of chocolate for dessert. I had no clue that it takes time to cook a chicken. I put the chicken in the oven at some high temperature and as soon as it looked nice and brown I declared it done. The whole meal was a disaster I was not aware of.

The next day Drasko bought me the *American Cook Book*. I studied it carefully and quickly learned the basics. What I did not learn is that people will not take second helpings unless they want to. So, at one dinner I prepared, nobody would have a second helping of the cake I made. I was convinced that something was wrong with the cake. After everybody left I dissected the cake and found white grains of sugar in the filling. My conclusion was that our guests thought those were some kind of bugs. I was horrified. Luckily I told the story to someone who explained to me that it is not rude not to take seconds when offered. Back home the hostess would insist you take seconds and you had better do it.

Val and Lia looked after us during our student years. They took us with them when Val and Drasko attended the conference in Washington, DC and in Boulder, Colorado. While the men were busy, Lia took me all over Washington in her convertible. In Boulder we joined a tour organized for spouses that took us to the Rocky Mountains ghost towns. Flying to Boulder (Denver) was my very first airplane travel. Both trips were extraordinary experiences for me. As far as I was concerned I saw the world.

Over the years we stayed in touch with the Telegdis. In the late sixties Val left the University of Chicago to be a professor at ETH, a university in Zurich, Switzerland, and to do experiments at CERN. They now live in Geneva, Switzerland.

++

An earthshaking event happened to me after school started in the fall of 1956. I received a thick envelope from the University Student Union. It was full of forms and questionnaires. My instant reaction was horror. I thought I had left all those organized intrusive groups back in Yugoslavia. I did not need a new form of organized control in my life. I thought that in America I was finally free to do whatever I wanted to. Nobody was to intrude into my private life again.

I asked Drasko what to do. He said to ignore the papers. I did not believe him. Then I asked a fellow student what he intended to do. He said he had no time to be bothered with those extracurricular activities. I asked him if it was permissible to ignore the summons. He looked at me like I was nuts. Nobody was going to tell him what he could or could not do. I finally understood that I could ignore the Student Union requests and that nobody was going to come to my door and arrest me. For the first time in my life I understood what freedom was.

++

The last big event in 1956 was the first Christmas reunion of our Yugoslav friends. Estie and Paul Murphy offered their home for the occasion. Marija and Boza Lalevic, Branka and Tosa Todorovic, Nidja Nikolic, Drasko and I, and Estie and Paul, spend a wonderful week together. We all appreciated the fact that we were not alone for the holidays away from home. The fact that December 25 was the wrong date for our Christmas did not bother anybody. Eastern Orthodox religion still uses the Julian calendar in which Christmas is on January seventh. I have to admit that I had no trouble adjusting to the Gregorian calendar. From that first Christmas in the United States we celebrated Christmas in December like everybody else.

The Yugo reunions, as we called them, became a regular event throughout the years to come. In 1957 Anica and Joca Jovanovic were in St. Louis, Missouri, and we all spent Christmas in their home. Later we had reunions in New York at the Todorovics; in Minneapolis at Vlada Skolnik's; at Forest Beach Camp in New Buffalo, Michigan; on Island Lake in Minnesota; in Cape May Point, where the Lalevics had a summer home; on Cape Cod; in Winnipeg, Canada; and in Driggs, Idaho.

Our latest reunion was in 2003, during the week of the 4th of July. It was also Marija and Boza Lalevic's fiftieth wedding anniversary. We were all there except for Vlada Skolnik. He passed away in 1990. The years had not changed us much. We were all still able to talk at the same time. Each one of us still believed that he or she knows everything, and that his or her opinion is the correct one and all others are wrong. The younger generation present thought we were all nuts. Well, we were all over seventy years old, and had the right to be right. We all hoped that this was not going to be our last reunion.

++

Drasko's father Dragoljub K. Jovanovic, Cika Dragi as I called him, came to visit us in July 1958. He was with us until October 5, 1958. Vera Laska helped us find a house for Drasko and me to housesit, while Cika Dragi stayed in our studio apartment. Professor Pierce Beaver, a University of Chicago professor of theology, and his wife Wilma were leaving for an extended trip to China and we got the use of their beautiful big house at the corner of Dorchester Avenue and 52nd Street.

Cika Dragi was excited about everything he saw: the way we lived, Lake Michigan, the walks in the neighborhood, Chicago and our friends. He went to St. Louis for a few days where Joca Jovanovic organized for him to give a talk at Washington University. My professor, Cyril Stanley Smith, and his wife Alice had us over one evening for dinner, served in their beautiful garden.

We took Cika Dragi to the Indiana Dunes State Park for a day's outing. We made him hike to the beach over a high dune. It was probably not easy for him to do, but he did not complain. We were too young to appreciate that at the time he was sixty-seven years old.

Cika Dragi did visit us two more times during his lifetime. In 1964 both he and Teta Mira, Drasko's mother, stayed with us for two months in Westmont, Illinois. Then in February 1968 Cika Dragi came from Paris where he had been an honored guest at the centennial celebration of Madame Curie's birth. He was one of the last three living colleagues of Madame Curie. At that time we lived in Downers Grove. Jasna was five and Vesna was a one year old.

While in Downers Grove, Cika Dragi did two major things. He translated Richard Feynman's book with six BBC lectures into Serbian and he sculptured in clay nearly life-size heads of Drasko, Jasna, Vesna and me. I am not sure that the Feynman book was ever published in Yugoslavia, due to copyright constraints.

I am sorry to say that we never fired our clay heads, and eventually they disintegrated.

We did see Cika Dragi in Belgrade one more time when Jasna, Vesna and I went to Yugoslavia for the first time in January 1969. He died in February 1970. Cika Dragi was a professor of physics at the University of Belgrade Physics Department and at the Medical School. He was a great man and a great scientist, loved by his family and by endless numbers of medical and physics students. For many years every doctor that graduated from Belgrade Medical School had to take Cika Dragi's physics course. And many Yugoslav doctors we met here in the United States knew Cika Dragi and remembered him with great respect.

The best part is that Cika Dragi liked me very much and thought I was smart. This is what he wrote in his diary on October 9, 1958, the day he left America:

"Stanka is a great person. She made it possible for me to meet many of her colleagues and others in her field, and to get familiar with the life of American researchers and professors. She is a realist and, I believe, is a perfect match for Drasko who is totally immersed in physics. Their life together is most beautiful, something I did not fully expect. She is a very intelligent, industrious and capable woman."

++

It took two years to complete the requirements for my Masters degree in Physical Chemistry. I graduated in June 1958, and then continued as a Ph. D. graduate student waiting for Drasko to finish his Ph. D. After Drasko graduated in 1959, we moved from our studio apartment to a modern one-bedroom apartment closer to Lake Michigan. With Drasko's post-doc salary we had more money than ever. We could afford to buy new furniture at "Accent," one of the first stores in Chicago to sell Danish furniture. We bought a couch, a drop-leaf dining room table that attached to a wall and four chairs, and a small coffee table. Today, Marina, my niece, has the dining room set, and the small coffee table sits next to Drasko's armchair in Urbana. A lesson: good furniture lasts forever.

The best part about the apartment was that it had floor heating. It was a new heating concept, with hot water pipes under the floor. We thoroughly enjoyed it. I went barefoot all winter long. There was also so much heat that we kept a window open all the time. We lived there until the summer of 1960 when we left Illinois and moved to California.

++

A green card was the most important piece of paper for foreigners who dreamed of living in the United States to have. It identified you as a permanent resident with all the rights of a citizen except for voting rights. To apply for a green card you had to have a job waiting for you. You also had to have an unblemished past.

The University of Chicago offered Drasko a postdoctoral position to follow his graduation in 1959. To be able to employ him, the University had to apply to the Immigration and Naturalization Service for permanent residency status for Drasko. The application automatically included an application for me, his wife. Soon after, we were invited for an interview. The interview was held in January 1959 in the INS Office, Room #908, 9th Floor, at 433 W Van Buren St. Chicago 7, Illinois. We were worried, but nowhere as concerned as we would have been if these were Yugoslav authorities interviewing us.

After the interview, we were asked to submit documents to prove that our past was clean. Branka Todorovic and Nidja Nikolic wrote affidavits that Drasko had served in the Yugoslav Army. The Chicago Police Department certified that we had "no arrests, convictions or sentencing to imprisonment." Similar statements were issued by the District Attorney's Office in Belgrade, Yugoslavia. Our University National Bank certified that we had money in the bank. All of $706.57.

A few months later we received our green cards in the mail. We were deliriously happy. Five years later, as soon as we had the right, we applied for American citizenship.

++

Did I miss my family back home? Yes and no. I had a strong desire to share my new life and all the experiences with them. I did it by writing long letters, very often, for many years. I typed them on my new Olympic typewriter, made carbon copies and mailed them to my father, to my mother and to Drasko's parents. In return my father wrote back as often as I did. My mother did too. Teta Mira, Drasko's mother, wrote often as well as my aunt Coka (my father's youngest sister) and my other aunts.

My close family was up-to-date on my life, and I was kept informed of happenings back home. I sent them many photos, and they sent many to me, too. Over the years my father, my mother, my aunt Coka and Drasko's parents came for extended visits. After 1969, Jasna, Vesna and I went several times for two-week visits to Belgrade. The last time I was in Belgrade was in 1988. From there I went to Hungary to attend a Dimitrijevic family reunion, organized by my cousin Aurel Hajto and me. Since then my brother Misa and my sister-in-law Irena have visited us several times. Their two sons Ivan and Marko now live in the United States.

Drasko and I had, and still have, a very close-knit life together. We did not really need anybody else to feel complete. We were always happily busy with our studies, with our research, and then later with our children. Life was, and is, very good to us.

LIVING IN PARADISE
1960–1962

In the spring of 1960 it was time for Drasko to look for a new job. He had several job offers and decided to take a position as the assistant research physicist at the brand new Department of Physics at the University of California San Diego in La Jolla, California. The main attraction was that Bob Swanson was already there, as were several other University of Chicago faculty members.

The next thing we did was buy a car. Drasko passed the driving test and I did not. Sometime in August 1960 we started our trip across the country in our new white Ford Falcon. The trip was a monumental experience for both of us. The enormous distances, the beauty of the open plains, of the mountains and of the Pacific Ocean was somehow unexpected. I was overwhelmed, and I fell in love with the country all over again.

We stopped at the Badlands. We stayed for several days in the Black Hills where we went on several hikes, saw Mt. Rushmore and swam in the hot springs. Somewhere along the road we nearly took a photo of a life-size "stuffed" buffalo and me. Unfortunately the buffalo moved his head and looked at me. He scared me to death and I ran for my life.

From the Black Hills we drove through the Big Horn Mountains on to Yellowstone National Park. We stayed for three days at the Yellowstone Hotel at Yellowstone Lake. That gave us enough time to hike to the top of Mt. Washburn, to visit a number of geyser basins and Yellowstone Canyon.

Brown bears were everywhere. I thought they were very cute. At one point we stopped along the road for me to feed them sugar cubes. I opened the car window half way and one bear hooked his claws on the glass pane and poked his head into the car. I gave him a sugar cube while Drasko took the picture. When we tried to drive away the bear would not let go of the window. We panicked and dragged the poor bear for several yards. He finally let go. Did I ever try to feed a wild animal again? Never.

On our last day in Yellowstone, August 23, 1960, we woke up to four inches of snow on the ground. The beauty of the country under the fresh snow was beyond description. But by noon it had all melted away.

From Yellowstone we drove south to Grand Teton National Park. The visual impact of what we considered real mountains hit us full force. We immediately decided to hike up to the top of the Grand Teton. At home in Yugoslavia there was always a secured trail up every peak for regular hikers to take. We assumed there would be one here, too. We stopped at the ranger station at Jenny Lake to get a trail map. The ranger took one look at us and suggested we go to Exhume climbing school and talk to them. We did and promptly dismissed them as a bunch of pompous rock climbers. We decided to find our own trail. We hiked up to Amphitheater Lake and crossed over the saddle toward the Teton Glacier on our way to the peak. The trail we followed quickly disappeared into nothing and we got properly scared. Never again did we attempt to hike peaks that did not have marked trails for hikers.

From the Tetons we drove to Salt Lake City via beautiful blue Bear Lake. In Salt Lake City we discovered the existence of Mormons. We did the tour of the Temple Square guided by a wealthy industrialist who volunteered his time. I could not believe half the things he told us. The concepts of prophets, the afterlife and polygamy were totally foreign to me. My little world consisted of Eastern Orthodox religion, the right one, and Roman Catholic religion, the wrong one. It took me a long time to learn and accept that there were many religions in the world.

After swimming, or I should say floating, in the Great Salt Lake we drove to Reno, Nevada. There we saw in performance Dean Martin, the vocalist, and Lily St. Cyr, the naked dancer dancing with feathers. In their own ways both were quite impressive. From Reno we visited Virginia City, a ghost town from the gold rush era. Then we drove to the beautiful, crystal clear Lake Tahoe. We stayed for a couple of days in a motel on the beach on the California side. We swam, drove around the lake and visited Squaw Valley, the site of the 1960 Olympic games.

We were then on our way to Berkeley, California, to visit Estie and Paul Murphy and their new baby Pamela. The Murphys took us around San Francisco, all beautiful and impressive. Soon we were on our way to La Jolla via US 1 and its unbelievably beautiful scenery.

++

What commenced were two years of the most beautiful weather in the most beautiful environment. We lived on the shores of the blue Pacific Ocean in a perpetual summer, with endless sunny days, and a profusion of flowers everywhere.

The new University of California San Diego campus was built around the old Scripps Institute for Oceanographic Studies and its aquarium. My laboratory was in a building hanging over a gorgeous sandy beach. Every day at noon I walked down a few steps to a changing room to get into my swimming suit, and then a few more steps down to the beach. Or, I just stepped outside to a garden lawn overlooking the ocean where lunch tables were set for us to enjoy. A long pier jutted out into the ocean where you could watch a variety of sea life playing in the water. If you did not see all you wanted to see looking into the ocean, you stepped into the aquarium and you got your fill of colorful sea life.

The new three-story science building was next door. The faculty and graduate students (there were no undergraduates in those days) congregated on the lawn or on the beach. Within days we had met practically everybody, and quickly developed a circle of new friends.

In addition to Bob and Jamie Swanson there were Gilbert (Gil) and Eva Clark, James (Jim) and Klonda Ball, William (Bill) and Jane Frazer, David and Kathy Wong, Gordon and Lorna Shaw and many more. We were similar in age and career stages. The men were all physicists. What the majority of us had in common was a love for hiking. A group developed that started going to the Sierras, or other closer mountains for weekend hikes.

Very soon after we arrived in La Jolla, Drasko had to go to Lawrence Berkeley National Laboratory in Berkeley, California. While there, he went to the Sierra Club store and bought hiking and camping equipment for us. We became owners of a lightweight two-person orange tent, Italian hiking boots with rubber soles (a great advancement in hiking boots) and two down sleeping bags. This was our very first purchase of luxury items that we could barely afford. They gave us the ability to hike and camp to our hearts' content. During the two years in La Jolla, we hiked in Yosemite National Park, Kings Canyon, Sequoia National Park, around Mt. Whitney, Mt. San Jacinto, Big Bear Mountains, Anza Borego desert, Joshua Tree National Monument and many more places.

Travel was easy since the weather was perfect all the time. The coastal fogs would roll in in the morning, but would quickly burn away. Once we camped in Yosemite Valley and woke up to a foot of snow. Instead of waiting for it to melt away we packed our gear and drove down to a lake on a lower elevation. There we spent the rest of the day swimming instead of hiking. Life was easy and very pleasant.

Drasko and I decided to spend the 1961 Christmas in Las Vegas. We found ourselves in the midst of the amazing entertainment and gambling world. For us it was more entertainment and very little gambling. There was Harry James and his band playing in the lobby of a big hotel. We saw Red Skelton, Mitzi Gaynor and the Moulin Rouge Review in various show rooms. For a few minutes we were in the same place as Elvis Presley (who was not much taller than me) and his entourage. Everything was glitzy and glittery, and neon lights were everywhere. We did manage, though, to tear ourselves away to visit Lake Mead, and to tour the Hoover Dam.

Camping in the desert was a new experience for us. We were camping in Joshua Tree National Monument when the thermometer reached a hundred degrees. I had never been exposed to such high heat before and I got sunstroke. I suddenly felt very cold and spent the day in my sleeping bag trying to keep warm. By the next morning I was back to normal. We were there in March to see the desert bloom. Fields of orange California poppies covered the land. Flowers I had never seen before bloomed on the parched desert ground. It was a beautiful sight to see and appreciate.

San Diego and its environs offered many things to see and do. There was Coronado Island and its famous hotel, the zoo, the San Diego Bay full of Navy ships, great restaurants and great beaches. We even drove to Tijuana several times, just over the border in Mexico. The shops and the entertainment, mostly striptease joints, amidst a kind of poverty I had never seen before, did not impress me much. But our out-of-town guests wanted to go to Mexico, so we did.

We also visited Palomar and Wilson Observatories, which were within driving distance from La Jolla. Then there was Disneyland. In Pasadena we saw the Rose Parade. Never again did we see so much within a short span of two years.

++

During our first week in La Jolla we stayed in a motel close to the Cove, La Jolla's famous beach. The Cove was too small and crowded for our taste. Keith Bruckner, the Chairman of the Physics Department who hired Drasko, drove us around to show us areas where we could live. In retrospect, I realized that he was trying to tell us to buy a piece of land and build a house. There were new subdivisions being developed on the hills above La Jolla Shores. The prices must have been right. But we had no understanding that the thing to do was to buy, and not to rent. The area was growing fast and we would have made a lot of money in just two years of living there.

The concept of ownership of real estate simply did not exist in our minds. I do not believe I ever realized that many of our friends lived in homes they owned. We rented a two-bedroom apartment in La Jolla Hermosa. It was in a beautifully landscaped complex of apartments built for Naval officers. We were on the ground floor with a balcony surrounded by flowering bushes. Very soon we rented a piano for Drasko. Altogether, we were very happy.

We lived on the south end of La Jolla. The University campus was north of La Jolla. To get there we drove on La Jolla Boulevard through the center of town, and then down the hill to La Jolla Shores and the campus. All along the way the views of the ocean were beautiful and the town was picturesque. Every drive was a pleasure trip.

Wind and Sea was a beautiful beach close to our apartment in La Jolla Hermosa. All the shops we needed were also close by.

++

Drasko and I must have been the first Eastern Europeans to hit UCSD. As such we were a curiosity and were invited to parties at homes of Scripps Institute of Oceanography old-timers. We took it in stride and thought little of it. The most exotic evening for us was the 1960 election eve dinner at the home of Professor and Mrs. Roger Revelle. Professor Revelle was the director of the Scripps Institute. They had a beautiful home right on a sandy beach with a wall of windows overlooking the ocean. It was a long evening waiting for the election results that elected John F. Kennedy the President of the United States. What I will never forget is Professor Revelle telling me that I should never lose my beautiful accent. That crushed me. I was convinced that my English was perfect, and that I had no accent. Unfortunately, to this day my accent is still with me.

We had dinners at Professor Harold C. Urey and his wife Frieda's house. They lived just inside a canyon halfway down the hill from the center of town. At one of these dinners I was helping in the kitchen. Frieda was preparing the salad and I got a lecture on how to crisp a head of lettuce. You cut the stem out, fill the lettuce with cold water, let it stand and then rip the leaves into small pieces. I am still doing it the same way.

Dr. Urey, a Nobel Prize winner, as well as many of the other senior scientists at UCSD, had been involved in the war effort to develop the atomic bomb. As part of a television documentary on the history of the atomic bomb, Howard K. Smith, a well-known reporter and TV anchor, came to interview Dr. Urey. I witnessed the interview because it was held in the lab where I was working at that time. Watching the taping of the interview was very disappointing. The reporter would ask Dr. Urey a question. Halfway through the answer the director would stop the camera from rolling, and start from the beginning over and over again. It went like that for hours. When I finally saw the documentary on the TV it had exactly thirty seconds worth of Dr. Urey in it.

In the course of the day Mr. Smith and I talked and he proudly told me that he had been the first American reporter assigned to Tito's headquarters during WWII.

++

Looking back at our life in La Jolla, it seems to me that Drasko was most of the time at Brookhaven National Laboratory on Long Island, New York. His group was doing experiments at the Cosmotron accelerator there. I did not like very much living alone. I had a wonderful job, and lots of friends, but still I wanted Drasko at home. At the same time Drasko was not very happy working under Professor Oreste Piccioni.

Job offers started coming Drasko's way from other universities, which were looking for high-energy physicists. There were not many of them around in those days. My thoughts were that, if we are going to move from paradise on earth, we should live within twelve miles of an accelerator, and start having a decent family life. Any university job would again set us apart. Drasko would again spend most of his time at an accelerator. So, when Dick Lundy suggested to Drasko to come to Argonne National Laboratory in Illinois we decided to go. Dick was already at Argonne building the Zero Gradient Synchrotron, the next-generation accelerator that high-energy experimental physicists would flock to.

Thus, we left glorious Southern California life for the Midwest and a much richer family life. Most of our friends, however, managed to stay in California. The ones that did experiments at an accelerator spent the better part of the rest of their professional lives away from home. I was grateful that we ended up living close to two major accelerators during Drasko's professional life. He did all his experiments while living at home, and not away from the family, as the majority of high-energy experimental physicist did.

In retrospect, going to Argonne was the right decision. Ten years later when Fermi National Accelerator Laboratory was located and built in Batavia, Illinois Drasko was close by and could get involved from day one. And he did.

BACK TO CHICAGO AND JASNA'S ARRIVAL
1962–1966

In the early summer of 1962 we were driving across the country on our way from La Jolla, California, to Long Island, New York. Drasko's new job at Argonne National Laboratory was to start in September. In the meantime he was still going to work on the experiments with his UCSD group at the Brookhaven National Laboratory on Long Island.

We took the northern route. We drove north to Seattle, then across northern Washington, Idaho and Montana to Minneapolis, Minnesota. Then we drove south to Chicago. The Pennsylvania Turnpike took us from Chicago on to New York and to Long Island.

On the way we visited many great places. In California we toured San Francisco, then the Giant Redwoods, then Eureka. We crossed into Oregon on the way to Crater Lake. And what a lake! We rented a rowboat and floated on the glassy surface looking down tens of feet into crystal clear water. It was actually a ghostly experience and I was happy to get back onto the solid ground.

We cut back to the Oregon Coast where for miles the road meandered parallel to the beautiful coast. Then we turned inland to Corvallis and Portland. All I remember of Portland from that trip was a city park set aside for homeless people to use. I am sure we did sightsee the town, but I do not remember any of it.

From Portland we drove to Mt. Rainier. We camped for a couple of days close to Paradise Inn. We thought we would hike a bit, but did not get far on the glaciers and the snow. The weather was superb. A year or so later I read in *National Geographic* about a group of climbers that were in training on Mount Rainier that summer. They were to climb the Himalayas later that year. During their six weeks of training they had a total of three clear, sunny days. Those were the two days when we were there, and the third day when we had a glorious view of Mt. Rainier from the Space Needle at the World's Fair in Seattle. We could not have been luckier.

The World's Fair was a special treat for us. We had never seen anything like that before. There were pavilions from all over the world with entertainers in native folk clothes performing native music and native dances. There was even a Yugoslav pavilion, totally unreal to us. We had dinner in the Space Needle restaurant and I felt I was on top of the world.

From Seattle we were on US 2 on the way to Spokane. We drove through the beautiful Cascade Mountains. Somewhere along the road we stopped for a swim in the blue-green crystal clear Columbia River. We stayed in Spokane overnight. The next day we continued on US 2 to Glacier National Park.

What impressed me the most in Glacier National Park were the paved roads. Anyone old and young could drive up to high altitudes and then take easy walks around. I attributed this to goodhearted Americans who made sure that even old people could enjoy being high up in the mountains. It did not occur to me that the roads had to go over high passes to get to the other side of the mountain range. Instead, I was happy to have nice thoughts about the goodness of Americans. We did hike to a glacier and took a boat ride on a big lake.

Our next stop was Minneapolis, where we visited our old friend Vlada Skolnik. From there we drove to Chicago. I do not remember where we stayed, but I am pretty sure we were looking at apartments to rent in the fall. The Lundys were living in the high-rise apartments in the middle of 55th street close to the University of Chicago. When we came back in September we decided to live there too.

From Chicago we drove straight to Long Island. We rented a small house very close to Smith Point beach. While Drasko drove to Brookhaven National Laboratory and was busy doing experiments, I walked to the beach and had a great summer. Our old friends Anica and Joca Jovanovic were also at Brookhaven that summer. Goran, their little boy was probably a year old. We saw a lot of them. Branka and Tosa Todorovic and their little boy Mark came from New York to visit us several times

Anica taught me how to make "ajvar," an eggplant relish. We made tons. I took ten big jars back to Chicago in the trunk of our car. On the drive back the days were hot. The heat fermented the relish and all ten jars exploded and made a gigantic mess in the trunk. My mild effort to expand my cooking skills backfired.

++

We arrived in Chicago at the beginning of September 1962. We moved into a one-bedroom apartment on the 8th floor of the ten-story high-rise building in the middle of 55th Street in Hyde Park. I loved it. We had wall-to-wall floor-to-ceiling windows in the living room and the bedroom facing south. We were higher then any other building for miles. Our view was spectacular. It somehow made up for not living in California anymore. We adjusted to our new life very quickly. Basically we came back to the same life we had before we left for California.

Argonne National Laboratory was thirty miles west of Hyde Park. It took Drasko over an hour to drive to work. There were no expressways in those days. Drasko drove on 55th Street for miles, and then on side roads to the lab. The Lundys were first to move closer to Argonne. They first rented and then bought a house in Downers Grove, a town twenty-five miles west of Chicago. We followed them a few weeks later. We rented a small three-bedroom house in Westmont, eleven miles north of Argonne. We lived there from the fall of 1963 until the spring of 1966 when we finally bought our first house and moved to Downers Grove.

++

Once back in Chicago I decided it was time for Drasko and me to start a family. I decided to get pregnant on September ninth, the same day our medical insurance was activated. Nine months later, on June 5, 1963, our daughter Jasna Diane was born at the University of Chicago Lying-In hospital. I was convinced she was the most beautiful baby ever to be born.

My father, Milos Dimitrijevic, spent six month with us while I was pregnant. I purposely sent him home one month before Jasna was born. I wanted Drasko and I to be alone when the baby arrived. It was a good decision.

When my father was with us we had enough money to afford to go to theaters, movies and restaurants. That was the year we saw the Bolshoi Ballet for the first time. We sampled a variety of restaurants that had been too expensive for us while we were students. We also had a car so we could explore Chicago and its environs. My father was mesmerized with it all. I remember he could not believe he could eat as many mushrooms as he liked. They were a great delicacy back home.

My father and I read the only book on pregnancy that I could find in those days. All of it was new to me and, to my greatest surprise, to him too. One simply did not talk about pregnancies back home. Actually, I am convinced I have never seen a pregnant woman in Yugoslavia. It was probably shameful to be seen with a big stomach.

On the way back to Yugoslavia my father visited the Lalevics in Philadelphia. Then he toured Washington, DC on his own. In New York he stayed with the Todorovics, who made sure he got aboard the S.S. Queen Mary that took him back to Europe and home.

That was the only time my father came to visit us in America. He had a great time and a nice visit with us. He met and liked all of our friends. Ivan Stojanovic, my father's cousin, his mother's oldest brother's son, came from Canada to visit him. It was a warm reunion after twenty years of separation. I truly believe my father went home happy and full of pleasant memories.

++

Some time in the morning of June 4, 1963 I started having labor pains. We went to the University of Chicago Lying-In hospital and I checked in. A short while later my pains stopped. Drasko and I decided it was a false alarm and we turned around and left the hospital. We sat in a park across the street from the hospital waiting to see whether the pains would come back. After a while the pains started again and we walked back to the hospital. In the meantime the hospital staff had been frantically trying to find me. My doctor had come, and since I was nowhere to be found, she had left. For some reason it had not occurred to us to let somebody know we were leaving. We must have been too preoccupied with my labor pains to think straight. Once we were back in the hospital, it took sixteen hours for Jasna to be born on June 5th at 2 AM.

Those were the days when spinal block anesthesia was routinely given. It allowed you to watch your own delivery. I watched for a while until it became too gross. I did not see Jasna's arrival into the world. Instead, the spinal block gave me a miserable headache. I could not lift my head off the pillow during the whole ten days I was in the hospital. While in the hospital I did my best to learn how to breastfeed even though formula was much preferred by everyone.

Once at home I breastfed Jasna for three weeks. Then Drasko decided that Jasna was not getting enough food and he insisted we supplement her feeding with formula. Pretty soon Jasna was happily drinking formula and I stopped breastfeeding. That was also much easier on me, especially when Playtex plastic bottles appeared on the market and I did not have to boil glass bottles anymore. I also had a diaper service that made life easy.

The months that followed were wonderful. Paul and Estie Murphy, who were by then living in England, sent to Jasna an original Silver Cross perambulator. It was white and navy blue with oversized wheels. There were attachments that came with it: a white canopy, a diaper bag, a rain cover and a mosquito net. The buggy part was removable and it fit into the back seat of our car. The pram was the best gift ever. It was later used by Vesna and several other babies. This year, 2004, Marina, my niece, will use it for her baby that is due in June.

The pram made it easy and comfortable to go on long walks and to sit in the gardens of our apartment building. Later, when we moved to Westmont, I had Jasna nap outside in the pram in all weather. As a consequence, I believed, she was a healthy baby with rosy cheeks.

Within a few days after coming home from the hospital I received a large package. Frieda Urey and my friends back in La Jolla had held a baby shower for me that provided practically everything I needed for the baby. They truly surprised me. It made me feel humble and grateful that they did not forget me and cared enough to get together on my behalf.

++

We loved the little house we rented in Westmont. We had our own backyard and a garage. Great luxuries. The front yard was sloping down so it felt like we were living on top of a small hill. There were three bedrooms: one for Drasko and me, one for Jasna, and one was a guestroom. Cika Dragi and Teta Mira, Drasko's parents, stayed in it in 1964, and then my mother, Emilija (Mila) Mihailovic in 1965. Our family visits were always two to six months long. It simply did not make sense for them to come for shorter visits. First, the trips were too expensive to come more often. Second, we loved having our family with us.

Over the years the total duration of all different family members' visits put together was close to five years. Even though we lived far away from home Jasna and Vesna got to know their grandparents and my aunt Coka really well. They also learned enough Serbian language for Jasna to later do a part of her Ph.D. dissertation work in Yugoslavia, and Vesna to be able to communicate with her Bosnian refugee patients in her family practice in Portland.

Jasna was one year old when Teta Mira and Cika Dragi were with us in Westmont. Our back yard was a pleasant place to be. I cultivated a nice flower garden, Drasko took care of the grass, Jasna had her blow-up plastic swimming pool and with comfortable lawn chairs everybody was happy. Teta Mira took great pleasure in taking Jasna for long walks in her stroller. Jasna loved it too. The day we all went to the beach at the Indiana Dunes State Park Jasna started walking. It was a monumental achievement for all of us.

My mom spent six weeks with us in 1965. That was the summer when Liz Lundy organized a joint vacation for all of us in Estes Park,

107

Colorado. Jasna was two years old, my mom was fifty-nine, Drasko was thirty-five and I was thirty-four. Dick and Liz Lundy had Nell who was a one year old. Dick's sister came along too. We all stayed in a big house close to the Rocky Mountain National Park. There was a swimming pool on site we all enjoyed. Mutual babysitting made it possible for Drasko and me to do some hiking, too.

We did one family hike. Drasko and I dragged Jasna and my mom on a hike along Bear Lake. It was a very pretty hike that ended in a mild disaster. Jasna lost her teddy bear. Drasko immediately retraced our steps and did not find it. Then we stopped at the ranger station to register our loss. We were hopeful because at the station we saw a shelf full of lost and found toys. A ranger assured us that if Jasna's teddy was found they would mail it to us. Indeed, several days later when we got back home to Westmont a package with Jasna's teddy bear was waiting for us. This was one more event to add to my list of why the United States was a great country.

++

We drove from Westmont to Colorado on the old US 80, which was in those days a two-lane road. The first day we drove to Des Moines, Iowa, and the second to North Platte, Nebraska. In North Platte we stayed in a brand new Holiday Inn. It may have been the very first Holiday Inn in the country with a "holidome." I was properly impressed with the big swimming pool, the restaurant with plush velvet chairs and the luxurious rooms. My mother, fresh from Yugoslavia, was even more impressed. A stretch of brand new four-lane US 80 Highway began just beyond the Holiday Inn. I do not remember how long a distance we drove on it, but it was a real treat compared to the old two-lane road.

On the way back we stayed in Des Moines, Iowa, where Drasko remembers Jasna ducking her head under water for the first time in the motel swimming pool. We considered that a milestone in Jasna's life. She was two years old.

We drove to Colorado in our new burgundy colored Buick Regal. We had lived happily with one car, our white Ford Falcon, until one cold winter day in early 1965 when Jasna fell on her face with a stick in her mouth and perforated her upper palate. There was lots of blood and lots of crying. I telephoned Drasko at his Argonne office and could not find him to come home and take us to the emergency room. I panicked and called Dr. Clara Prec, Jasna's pediatrician, who promptly drove from her Downers Grove office to our house in Westmont and took care of Jasna. Jasna ended up with several stitches in her palate, and we ended up with a brand new second car. Never again was I alone with my children without a car.

++

Dusan (Dusko) Trbojevic, Drasko's mom's first cousin, and his wife Gordana were the only other relatives that visited us while we were in Westmont. Dusko was a well-known Yugoslav concert pianist. During his stay with us Ted Novey, a senior physicist and Drasko's group leader at Argonne, and his wife Elaine asked Dusko to play a concert in their home. There must have been fifty people at the Novey's listening to the wonderful concert Dusko performed. Drasko and I were very pleased and proud that a relative of ours, from the Balkans no less, was such a great artist.

++

A sad memory I have from the time we lived in Westmont was the assassination of President John F. Kennedy in November 1963. I was a happy mother of a five-month old baby Jasna when the tragedy hit. I just could not believe that something like that could happen in our wonderful United States. I was glued to the television for three whole days. After it was all over and the tragedy slowly started to fade away, I decided never again would I make myself miserable by watching tragedies unfold on the television. And I never did.

Over time there was other news that upset the nation. But, somehow, it did not emotionally touch me. There were Chicago riots, the civil rights movement, Vietnam War, Watergate and more. I followed all with interest as an observer. I was amazed that people could actually demonstrate at a major political party convention. I equated it with freedom. Martin Luther King Jr. and his valiant followers impressed me to no end, even though I knew very little about the history of slavery and the segregation problems in the country. The Vietnam War was too sad an affair that America did not seem to know how to get out of. I felt the Vietnamese people should solve their own problems. I felt that Watergate was a fiasco created by President Nixon, and his not very smart staff.

Somehow, my attitude was that there was little I could do to solve the world's problems. The best I could do was vote for good people that might make our world a better place.

++

In August 1964, after five years of having permanent residency status, we had the right to apply for American citizenship. And we did. Within a few weeks we were asked to come to the INS Office and take the exam on United States history and government. We had to know all about the different forms of government in use in the country: village, town, city, state and federal government. We had to know a bit of American history and name the presidents.

I still have the book we studied from. It was *Federal Textbook on Citizenship—Constitution and Government* by Catheryn Seckler-Hudson, Professor of Political Science and Public Administration Graduate School, at the American University. I bought it from the U. S. Government Printing Office for $1.25. I took the studying seriously and at that time I knew more about the United States Government than a majority of people born in this country. I found the American democratic form of government very appealing and was happy to adopt the country as my own. In return I felt that the country adopted me, too.

Drasko became a citizen on December 1, 1964 and I on January 12, 1965. To be an American citizen felt like being born again. Ever since I have been very proud to call the United States of America my country.

++

Bob and Jamie Swanson invited us to spend the 1964 Christmas holidays with them in La Jolla. We were happy to go back to the glory of Southern California even if it was only for a week. Many of our friends were still there. We stayed with Gil and Eva Clark who had a guesthouse attached to the house they were living in. At that time Lisa, their older daughter, was a new baby. The Swansons cooked the Christmas dinner. The rest of the time we did our own thing.

Jasna was the only unhappy member of our family. She developed a terrible ear infection. By the time we recognized what she was crying about and took her to the doctor her ears were inflamed. The doctor had to puncture her eardrums to drain them. It took six months, and two doses of antibiotics, until the infection was completely gone.

++

Westmont was one of many small towns located along various railroad tracks radiating out of Chicago. Westmont and Downers Grove were along the Burlington line. The towns were self-contained and pleasant to live in. The very first suburban shopping mall had just opened in Oak Brook, maybe ten miles away from us. We mostly shopped locally at the corner drugstore, a dime store, a general store and a small supermarket in town. There was a local bank, a dentist and an optometrist. For all other services we went to Downers Grove, five miles west of Westmont.

In those days I did all the housework, the shopping and the cooking. We bought a washer-dryer combination machine that made my life easier. We did not have a dishwasher until we moved to Downers Grove in 1966. A washing machine was essential because disposable diapers did not exist then. I did have a diaper service for a while longer, but it was not a cheap service. Once Jasna was a little older, I switched to cloth diapers I washed at home.

The nice thing about a small town is that you get to know your neighbors. The Grimm family next door to us had five children older than Jasna. The younger ones were Jasna's playmates, the older ones were her babysitters. In 1965, when I started working part time at Argonne National Laboratory, Dorothy Repiha, who lived a few houses down the street, baby-sat Jasna.

In the early spring of 1966, our landlord, a farmer and his wife, decided to move from their farm to town. They needed their house back. We again started looking for a house to rent and luckily, we could not find one. Finally, we were forced to look into buying a house. A realtor took us by the hand and led us step by step through the whole process. When we found the house we liked and could afford, it was inspected by an expert from Argonne National Laboratory. That was a free service the Laboratory provided for its employees. The house was structurally fine, and we liked the neighborhood very much. The best part was that the house was five blocks from the Lundys' house.

How we got the mortgage is a mystery to me. The realtor drove us in his car to a big bank in downtown Chicago. There we signed all sorts of papers and got a twenty-five year mortgage loan at 6% interest. I was hoping Drasko understood what we were doing, because I certainly did not. Just the concept of a mortgage was totally foreign to me.

++

We moved into our house at 4808 Wallbank Avenue in Downers Grove in June 1966. A couple of weeks later we left for Berkeley, California. Drasko was participating in a six-week workshop, the 200 GEV Design Study that ultimately created Fermilab. While Drasko worked, Jasna and I had fun. I had the car so it was easy to go places. Our favorite activity was going to the Strawberry Canyon swimming pool.

The three of us went on a memorable camping trip to Yosemite National Park. We camped on Tenaya Lake. The lake was warm enough to swim, a great pleasure for all three of us. We had a Sierra Club backpack for Drasko to carry Jasna, which made it possible for us to go for short hikes. We had our camping and hiking gear with us. It is still a mystery to me how we managed to bring all that camping equipment with us on our flight from Chicago.

Another adventure was going on a bus to Folsom Lake west of Sacramento to see one of the proposed sites for the future accelerator. After touring the site, which was nothing but farmland in the Sierra foothills, workshop participants and their families spent the rest of the day at Folsom Lake picnicking and swimming.

The International Conference on High Energy Physics, the "Rochester" Conference, was held that summer in Berkeley. Paul Murphy, from England, and Hans Sens, from Switzerland, attended the Conference. Hans came with his wife Graca, whom we had not met before. It was a happy reunion of old friends from the University of Chicago.

OUR FIRST HOUSE AND VESNA'S ARRIVAL
1966–1969

We finally owned our own home. It was a brick Cape Cod built in 1943. A combination living and dining room stretched out along the front of the house. It was a space thirteen by twenty-eight feet with the stairs at one end going to the second floor. A den, a kitchen and a bathroom completed the first floor. The upstairs had two bedrooms and a bath. There was also a partially finished basement. We had more room than ever before and it all belonged to us. That was a very peculiar sensation we quickly got used to.

The house was on a wide street shaded with old maples and oaks. Our large lot, sixty by two hundred and fifty feet, also had several old trees. We had a two-car garage, a nice patio in the back yard, plenty of room to play badminton and room for me to have a garden. Very nice people lived on the street. Next door to us were Betsy and Albert Ramp and their teenage children, Georgia and Albert, Junior. A few houses down the street were Dolores and John DeWitt. They had three young daughters, Cindy, Nancy and Janet; and Gloria and John Kazienko, who had four girls, Loretta, Christine, and a few years later, the twins, Dona and Theresa.

Nancy DeWitt and Loretta Kazienko were Jasna's age. They all three became great friends. Later Nancy and Jasna went to public schools, while Loretta was in a Catholic school. They were also Blue Birds together.

Living close to families with children of Jasna's age was great for both Jasna and me. When they played together I was free to do my work at home.

+ +

When Jasna was two, Drasko and I decided to have another child. To my great surprise I did not get pregnant for a full year. That was a major difference from getting pregnant with Jasna, which took one day. So, instead of being born in the spring of 1966, Vesna was born in the spring of 1967.

At the time I worked two days a week at Argonne National Laboratory. I went to work until the very last day of my pregnancy. On June 20, 1967, around 8 PM, I started having labor pains. This time I did not rush to the hospital. I took my time and calmly read to Jasna *Put Me In The Zoo* and *Little Black Pony*, as I did every evening at her bedtime. Then I called Dolores, our neighbor, to come over to take care of Jasna until Drasko came back from the hospital.

Drasko and I drove to Hinsdale Hospital in Hinsdale, Illinois, about ten miles away from our home. We got there by 11 PM and shortly after midnight I was in the delivery room. This time I had gas anesthesia that did not put me completely under, but kept me happy. By 1 AM on June 21, 1967 Vesna Ann was born. She was, like Jasna, the most beautiful baby ever born.

I was in the hospital for only three days. Vesna was on formula from the very beginning, which meant I could go back to work and not worry about breastfeeding. It took less than three weeks for our life to get back to normal. When Vesna was three weeks old, Dorothy Repiha was back babysitting, and I went back to work.

I got Jasna involved in taking care of Vesna from the day we came back from the hospital. She helped to feed and bathe Vesna. They slept in the same small bedroom upstairs and pretty soon Vesna was assimilated into our family without any jealousy or any other problems on Jasna's part.

++

Living in Downers Grove was very pleasant. The streets were lined with hundred-year-old oaks and maples. There were no fences, so the backyards were continuous parkland. Our Wallbank Avenue was only two blocks long, with very little traffic. It was safe for children to play with little supervision anywhere around the homes.

We became members of the Downers Grove Swim and Racket Club. The Club was in an old apple orchard, and had two swimming pools, a wading pool and several tennis courts. It was ten minutes away, across town from our home. The upper pool was a big square pool with one corner area three feet deep for younger children. Diagonally across was the corner set for diving. The rest of the pool was four feet deep, the main play area for children of all ages. Down a short incline there was an Olympic-size pool for serious swimming. To be allowed to use the lower pool children had to be able to swim two pool lengths. The children took great pride in passing the test, and then went back to the upper pool where the real fun was.

The swimming season was from Memorial Day to Labor Day. Jasna, Vesna and I went to the pool every afternoon. Many of their friends and my friends would be there, too. At around five in the afternoon most of the families went home for dinner. The three of us stayed to wait for Drasko, who came straight from work to join us. More often than not we ate dinner at the pool's small restaurant. We then stayed and swam until seven or eight in the evening. The best part was that at around dinnertime we practically had the pools to ourselves.

Drasko and I did try to learn how to play tennis. At our very first try, Drasko cut his left eyebrow with the racket. We ended up in the Hinsdale hospital emergency room, and never played tennis again.

++

The only big vacation we had in those days was going to Sanibel Island, Florida, in the spring of 1968. Our friends Nikola and Katica (Kaca) Sorak had been to Sanibel twice since they had arrived in the United States in 1962. Kaca and Nikola were much more adventurous than we were and thought nothing of driving long distances for short vacations. Their adventures in Florida, Colorado and the Bahamas gave us the impetus to go there too. We followed in their footsteps many times and were never sorry.

Nikola Sorak had been my brother Misa's best friend in elementary school in Belgrade. He and his wife Kaca looked us up when they arrived in Chicago in 1962. We have stayed good friends ever since. Nikola was an electrical engineer, and Kaca was a medical doctor. Eventually, they had three children, Danilo, Lillian and Philip. Today the Soraks live in Maggie Valley in North Carolina, in the hills close to Smoky Mountain National Park.

One of Kaca's colleagues vacationed on Eleuthera, in the Bahamas. The Soraks then went there, too. The first time they were there they bought a small house on the Caribbean side of the island. So, of course, we also had to go there. Unfortunately, we were not smart enough in those days to also buy a piece of property. But, that did not prevent us from spending several vacations in the Soraks' house in the years to come.

To go back to our first Sanibel vacation, Jasna was nearly five years old and Vesna was nine months old. The island was not commercialized yet. We stayed in a beach cabin at one of the few motels there. We had a long, nearly wild beach to ourselves. There was also a nice swimming pool right off the beach. The beach was peppered with live and dead shells of all kinds. We all loved to collect them, and we brought a great shell collection home with us. To this day shelling is still one of our favorite beach activities.

We vacationed on Sanibel two more times, in 1970 and 1973. Jasna and Vesna were older, so we could do more exploring. We went to Naples, to Marco Island and to Captiva, where at the resort restaurant I had a cherry jubilee, my very first flaming dish. We also hired a motorboat and explored several wild islands north of Captiva. In the sixties and early seventies when we were there, all these places had just begun to develop, or were totally wild. Again, I was not smart enough to buy a piece of real estate. In retrospect, I wish I had known better.

++

In May 1968, Drasko's brother Manojlo (Leka), his wife Branka and their three-year-old son Dejan came from Yugoslavia for a visit. It was the first time the brothers had met since Drasko left for America in 1954. Leka was a forestry engineer working in the paper industry back home in Belgrade. When he discovered how easy it would be for him to change his profession by going to graduate school in the United States, he decided to try it. Leka was an avid fisherman and had always wanted to study fishery biology. But there was no such course back home. He applied to be a graduate student and was accepted in the Department of Fishery Biology at the University of Michigan.

We were delighted that he would remain in this country, but were sad to see Branka and Dejan go back home to Yugoslavia. There was no way for them to stay with Leka at that time. He was going to be a very poor and a very busy graduate student.

On the other hand, Branka had a good job at home that she could not just leave. She had a degree in English Language and was teaching at the Yugoslav Airlines Training Center in Belgrade. It was her job that made it possible for their family to travel on free airline tickets. Otherwise they would have never been able to come to visit us in the first place.

Finally, in May 1970, Branka and Dejan joined Leka in Ann Arbor, Michigan. A year later, in August 1971, Leka, with a Master of Science degree to his name, got a job in Chicago. In 1975 they bought a house in Wheeling, Illinois, where Branka, now a widow, still lives.

For Jasna and Vesna and for Dejan, and later for his sister Marina, living close by was the best thing that could have happened to them. Having an extended family while growing up enriched their lives beyond what Drasko and I could have done alone. Our families spent many holidays and vacations together. The children developed great friendships that stayed with them forever. Today they and their families make a point of getting together at least twice a year for several days of love, fun and games.

++

In August 1968 Drasko and Dick Lundy were at a conference in Vienna, Austria. Drasko decided that the political situation in Yugoslavia had changed for the better and that it would be okay for him to travel to Belgrade to visit his parents. To be on the safe side he asked Dick to come with him. Drasko believed that if the Yugoslav authorities tried to detain him in Belgrade, Dick would be able to help him get out of the country.

The visit was a very pleasant one. After fourteen years of being away, Drasko was with our families again. I am sure the trip was pretty exotic for Dick. He can still tell a story or two about their adventures there.

Drasko's trip to Yugoslavia broke the ice for me, too. He was traveling with an American passport and had no problems entering or leaving the country. No one from the Yugoslav authorities came looking for him. He felt free to go anywhere he wanted. So, in early January 1969, when we were on the way to England for Drasko's sabbatical at the University of Manchester, Jasna, Vesna and I detoured and flew to Belgrade. We spent a wonderful two weeks with our families. None of them, except Drasko's father, had yet met Vesna, and most of them had never met Jasna either. There was love and tears of joy in abundance. We happened to be there for our Eastern Orthodox Christmas on January 7. To Jasna and Vesna's delight, my father recreated a true traditional Eastern Orthodox Christmas, with a Christmas tree decorated with candles, sparkles and old-fashioned candies.

We visited my mother and Cika Bora, my stepfather, often. They lived in a very nice apartment several trolley bus stations away. We spent time with Cika Dragi and Teta Mira, Drasko's parents. Tetka Cicika and Cika Cveta, my aunt and uncle, came from Zmajevo. Coka, my youngest aunt, came from Sombor for the duration of our stay in Belgrade. Somebody drove us to Pancevo to visit Tetka Beba, my father's oldest sister, Teca Laza and my cousin, Ksenija Ilijevic. Many other relatives stopped by to see us.

My brother Misa's law office was in my father's apartment at Terazije 1 where we were staying. We saw Misa daily. Jasna and Vesna quickly got used to the idea that everybody who came to the front door was a relative to be kissed and hugged. It took some explaining to convince them that Misa's clients, who arrived at the front door a few days later, were not the family. Some of them did get a few kisses and hugs anyway.

Only Misa knew enough English to communicate with Jasna and Vesna. We somehow never had bothered to teach our children any

Serbian. We were so proud of being English-speaking Americans that we simply gave up on the Serbian language. We believed that we would never need it again. That was a major mistake on Drasko's and my part. Later, the girls learned enough Serbian to be able to communicate from Coka and their grandparents, who stayed with us for extended visits.

Parting was sad but the knowledge that we would come again made it easier on everybody. And we did come again many times, while Drasko's and my parents, and my aunts were alive. My last visit to Yugoslavia was in 1988.

LIFE AT HOME AND ABROAD
1969-1975

Paul G. Murphy, Professor of Physics at the University of Manchester in Manchester, England, and our old friend from the University of Chicago days, invited Drasko to spend a sabbatical year at his university. Drasko accepted, and took a six-month sabbatical leave from Argonne National Laboratory. Thus, we spent January to June 1969 in Manchester, England.

Drasko flew directly to England while Jasna, Vesna and I detoured to Yugoslavia to visit our families. While we were in Yugoslavia, Drasko was to find an apartment or a house for us in Manchester. It did not work out that way. He could not find a place to rent that had a decent heating system.

To Paul and his wife Estie's delight, we had no choice but to live with them in their big house throughout our stay in England. Not only did we stay with them, but my aunt Coka came from Yugoslavia and spent two months with us, too. The house at 35 Belfield Road in Didsbury, in Manchester, was pretty big. It had central heating that replaced eleven boarded-up fireplaces. There was enough room for all of us.

Pamela and Bryan, Paul and Estie's children, were in school most of the day. Jasna was in first grade at Beaver Road Church of England School, across the street from our house. Estie was attending a local college working toward a teaching degree in biology. She had a degree in physical education from the United States, but needed a British degree to be able to teach. Drasko and Paul went to the University, or to the Daresbury Laboratory outside of Manchester, where they did experiments at the 5GeV electron synchrotron called NINA. Vesna and I stayed home and had fun.

It was very quickly clear to me that I was not going to be able to cook for all of us. There was no abundance of meat available at the butchers, the main staple of my cooking. Estie slowly took over the cooking and produced great meals with little or no meat. There were varieties of odd sausages that we regularly ate. Big roasts, and other meat dishes, were weekend fare. Estie was also a wizard in producing desserts and other dishes the children liked. I ended up setting the table, cleaning after the meals and doing the dishes. There was really very little else I could do.

Estie had a cleaning woman, an ironing woman, a scrubbing woman and a gardener, who came regularly. The social structure was so pronounced in England at the time that even the hired help was stratified. The ironing woman was above the cleaning woman who was above the scrubbing woman. Where the gardener fell I did not even bother to find out. Coming from America, not to mention socialist Yugoslavia, the social structure seemed ridiculous.

Paul and Estie made sure that we did plenty of sightseeing. They took us, or told us where to go. We visited Chester, castles in Wales, Blackpool, the moors where The Bronte sisters' house was and Chatsworth castle. We also toured Liverpool, Cambridge, Oxford, London and much more. We spent the Easter holiday with Paul's parents, Alfred and Helen Murphy. They lived at Cayley Lodge in Cranfield, Berkshire. Alfred Murphy was the vice-chancellor of Cranfield Institute of Technology, which later became a university. They lived in the chancellor's house. It was a big house with many bedrooms, a Swiss butler and a housekeeper. For three days we lived the way the British nobility must have lived. I was properly impressed with it all.

Drasko and I went to Paris, France for a long weekend. We left Jasna and Vesna in Coka and Estie's care. While in Paris we made it a point to visit the Curie Institute where, as the son and the daughter-in-law of Professor Dragoljub K. Yovanovitch, as they spelled his name, we were warmly received. We were there soon after the Centennial Celebration of Madame Curie's birth at which Drasko's father was an honored guest. He was Madame Curie's student in the early 1920s, received his doctorate degree from the Paris University-Sorbonne and then worked with Madame Curie until 1929. In 1968 he was one of the three surviving collaborators of Madame Curie. To our chagrin the film in our camera did not roll. All the great photos we thought we took did not happen.

Drasko, Jasna and I also spent several days in Switzerland. We left Vesna in Coka and Estie's care. We went to visit Hans and Graca Sens, and their twin girls, who lived outside of Geneva. Hans, a professor at Utrecht University in Holland, and an old friend from University of Chicago days, was doing experiments at CERN. We toured Geneva, than drove to Bern, and then on to Lucerne. We spent a couple of days in a hotel on Lake Lucerne where Queen Victoria had vacationed many years before us. From there we drove to Grindelwald, where we took the funicular up the Jungfrau Mountain, 13,642 feet high. Then back to Geneva.

Paul and Estie made us feel at home. We were one big happy family. Estie was and is by nature a happy person full of joy that somehow transferred to all of us. Their hospitality transcended all the bounds of friendship. To this day we are very grateful.

++

A couple of weeks after we returned to Downers Grove we repacked and flew to Aspen, Colorado. Drasko was participating in a workshop that was planning future Fermilab experiments. Robert R. Wilson, Fermilab Director, was from Wyoming. He believed that the physicists did their best thinking when they were in the mountains. Thus, many workshops, program committee meetings and study groups were held in Aspen and in Snowmass.

As early as 1969 there were condo complexes in Aspen where large number of physicists and their families could stay. In the coming years new condo complexes were built and the accommodations became more and more luxurious. Our favorite was Roaring Fork condos, where the apartments hang over the roaring Roaring Fork creek. The swimming pool and the Jacuzzi added to our pleasures.

The meetings were organized in such a way that there was always time for hiking, fishing and other fun. On some days, the afternoon meetings were moved to the evenings. Family and friends had time to spend together hiking, fishing, or just sitting around the swimming pool and talking. The big hiking trips were left for the weekends.

There were also social events organized by Fermilab for the participants and the families. A big picnic was held in the Ashcroft Valley, next to a ghost town where the children had a great time.

While Jasna and Vesna were too little to hike, we would drive up into the mountains somewhere, pitch the tent next to a creek and spend the day playing. Once in a while Drasko and I would do a bigger hike and leave the children with a babysitter. On later trips to Aspen when Vesna was six or so, we started taking them on short hikes. Eventually, they learned to love hiking, and today they are both great hikers.

On July 20, 1969 we drove from Aspen to Leadville for a day of sightseeing. It was the day Apollo 11 landed on the moon. We were driving and listening to the lunar landing transmission on the car radio. This was a monumental event for me. The Apollo 11 flight was bringing the lunar samples back that my colleague George Reed and I would study. With the history of the American West all around us, and the looming future of the space exploration happening at the same time, we had a quite unforgettable day.

Often we would stay a few extra days after the meetings were over. I discovered there was a Mr. Alfred Braun in Aspen who took care of the ski-touring huts in the area. The huts were closed during the summer months, but I talked Mr. Braun into letting us use one. Tagert Hut was located above the Ashcroft Valley on the way to Montezuma mine. We paid three dollars per person per night to stay there. The hut had a cooking stove and mattresses on the floor. We had our camping gear and used the hut as a shelter. The day hikes from the Tagert Hut were great. The hut was at 11,250 feet altitude in the Pearl Basin below the Pearl Pass. Gorgeous country and nobody there but us.

Most of the time we drove back home to Illinois the long way. At different times we drove via the Grand Teton and Yellowstone National Parks, via Crested Butte and the Black Canyon of the Gunnison, via Ouray, Silverton and Telluride, via Rocky Mountain National Park, via Flaming Gorge National Recreation Area and via many other routes. On the way we would stop to visit museums, historical places, ghost towns, hot springs and other attractions. These trips were always educational and great fun.

The best part about all of these summer vacations was that Fermilab defrayed some of the costs. We paid very little for accommodations, if at all. So, thanks to Drasko's physics and Fermilab we spent many great summer vacations in Aspen. The only thing I regret is that I was not knowledgeable enough in the early seventies to realize that we should have invested in real estate in the area. By the time I knew we should have done it, it was too late. A thirty thousand dollar condo in 1974 was a quarter million dollars ten years later. By the mid-eighties we were priced out of every mountain resort area in Colorado. Luckily, when in 1987 we discovered Teton Valley, Idaho, still reasonably priced, we bought without hesitation a small house on 2.7 acres of land. And we did the right thing. Today, we would be priced out from there too.

+++

In the summer of 1969 we discovered the YWCA Forest Beach Camp on Lake Michigan, in New Buffalo, Michigan. Adjacent to the YWCA sixty-four acres girls' camp there were three summer cottages available for rent. The cottages were on a high dune above the lake and its beautiful sandy beach. There was a two-bedroom smaller cottage, a two-bedroom big cottage, and a three-bedroom very big cottage. Over the years, we stayed in all of them. Most of the time we were in the middle cottage. Adults slept in the bedrooms, and the children slept on the screened porch overlooking the lake. Actually, grownups enjoyed sleeping on the porch, too.

Jasna and Vesna always brought friends. Leka, Branka, Dejan and Marina often came with us. Other friends came for a day or two.

Whoever was visiting from Yugoslavia at the time would come with us. My mom, Teta Mira, Coka and Misa vacationed with us there. Invariably everybody loved it. The days were spent on the beach, playing in the sun, swimming or just sun bathing. Drasko had his minifish sailboat with him, and the younger people had fun sailing. We were always there for the last two weeks in August when the weather was great.

In the late seventies the YWCA decided to close the cottages. Their budget could not cover the cost of their upkeep. To preserve our vacation haven for us, I offered to organize a group of volunteers to do the annual upkeep. The Camp Director agreed, and for several years our family and friends spent the Memorial Day weekend cleaning, painting and doing minor maintenance of all three cottages. We continued this until sometime in the mid-eighties, when the camp, including the cottages, was sold to a developer. We lost a wonderful vacation place.

We moved our Lake Michigan vacations to Gintaras resort, a few miles north in Union Pier. The resort had a main house and a lodge, and several cabins. The owners Mr. And Mrs. Algirdas and Victoria Karaitis, originally from Lithuania, made the resort friendly and pleasant for the guests. The beach was beautiful and we loved it there.

In addition to our regular vacations, two other major events happened at Gintaras. In August 1986, a week-long reunion of our old Yugoslav friends was held there. Then, on June 19, 1992, Jasna and Tom were married there. Their wedding was a three-day celebration with family and friends. We had the whole resort to ourselves with over ninety guests who came from all over the United States and Europe.

Drasko and I continued to spend our two weeks at the dunes until Drasko retired in 1997. Once we stopped working, we spent summers in Driggs, Idaho, and winters in Florida. Our Lake Michigan vacations became a wonderful memory.

‡

In the summer of 1971, we did our big trip to Europe, and we went to Yugoslavia again. The four of us flew to Geneva, Switzerland, where we visited Hans and Graca Sens for several days. Then we rented a Mercedes, a very luxurious car for us, and began our three-week trip. We traveled to Interlaken in Switzerland, via Goddard Pass to Lago Maggiore and Venice in Italy. Then we crossed into Yugoslavia and drove on to Porec, Pula, Opatija, Plitvice Lakes, Zagreb and then to Belgrade. From Belgrade we made a short trip to Drasko's family's summer home in Soko Banja.

The beauty of the countryside we traveled through was overwhelming. We saw the Swiss and Italian Alps; the endless Lago Maggiore; Venice with its architecture, canals and romance; Miramar palace outside of Trieste, and its beautifully tiled visitors' bathroom without toilets, just holes, and stalls without doors; then in Yugoslavia the coliseum in Pula; then Magistrala, the highway hugging the shores of the blue Adriatic Sea; and then we went through the Velebit mountains to the seven lakes and waterfalls at Plitvice Lakes.

After two weeks of visiting our families in Belgrade we were back on the road again. We drove to Slovenia, where we spent several days at Bled on beautiful Lake Bled. We rented a rowboat and visited the church on the small island in the middle of the lake. We went to Vintgart canyon, and we swam in the lake and in our hotel's indoor swimming pool. Then we drove through Kranjska Gora, where I had vacationed in my youth, to Vrsic Pass. The pass was in the heart of Julian Alps with many peaks I had hiked when I still lived in Yugoslavia. The road took us to the spring of the Soca River, a blue pool of water in a hole deep in the ground. Once we left the Julian Alps behind, we drove straight back to Geneva. Seeing, on the way, the Italian Alps and Mont Blanc was an additional bonus.

In those days we were pretty rich by European standards. We could afford to stay in luxury hotels, and we did. I was most impressed with the hotels' bathrooms. In Venice we had a black tile bathroom where the corner shower sprayed directly into the room. By the time we figured out how to use it the whole bathroom was soaking wet. At the Plitvice Lake hotel there must have been ten showerheads shooting at you from above, below and from several protruding side arms. The water was not easy to control, and we were hit with hot and cold water, but mostly cold. The hotel also had a number of stuffed wild animals all over the place that took you by surprise.

A year later, in November 1972, I took Jasna, Vesna and Dejan, their cousin, to Yugoslavia for a visit. It was a big event for my father because we were there for Slava, my family's patron saint Archangel Michael's day, on November 21. The traditional customs were observed. The priest came to bless the house and the Slava cake. Tetka Katica, my stepmother, prepared traditional dishes, including a roasted suckling pig. Jasna, Vesna and Dejan were especially impressed with the suckling pig's head on the platter.

While we were in Belgrade, Marina, Dejan's sister was born on November 26 in Highland Park, Illinois. The telegram we received somehow misspelled Marina's name, and for a while we were not sure whether the newborn was a boy or a girl. Finally, I telephoned Drasko, a very expensive thing to do then, and found out for sure that Dejan had a new sister.

⧻

After we came back from Europe in July 1973, we were again off to Aspen for Drasko to attend a Fermilab workshop. My brother Misa came to visit us in August. This was his first trip to America. Misa flew directly to Aspen. We were staying in a Roaring Fork condo, in luxury that did not exist in Yugoslavia. Misa loved it. While Drasko was working, Misa, Jasna, Vesna and I had a great time. We played in the swimming pool, sat in the Jacuzzi, went up the mountains on the ski lifts and did lots of sightseeing.

The most memorable thing we did was to go horseback riding, a very unsuccessful undertaking. The man at the stable helped us mount the horses and then left the area. Other riders took off up the mountain trail, while the four of us, who knew nothing about horses, were still in the corral. Our horses would not budge and we had no idea how to make them move. I gave up and somehow got off my horse. Then I struggled to separate Jasna and Vesna's horses so that they could get off. While I was doing that Misa's horse trotted away to a pile of hay some distance from the corral. By the time we caught up with Misa his horse was happily munching hay, totally ignoring Misa who was stuck on top of him. Finally Misa got off and we drove away leaving the horses unattended. In sheer frustration we ended up laughing hysterically. To this day I have a clear picture in my head of Misa sitting on top of the horse while it ate hay, and I laugh all over again.

Another adventure was taking Misa camping. Misa, a lawyer and a totally city person, good-naturedly went along with our plans. He slept on the ground in the tent then he hiked an hour or so up to Maroon Lake, and back down. By the time we got back home he was totally exhausted. The poor man was boiling hot all day. We did not think of telling him how to dress for the day. Early in the morning it was cold at the campsite. So, he put his hiking clothes on over the warm pajamas he slept in. The day became hot and hiking in all those clothes nearly did him in. We got a good laugh out of that adventure, too.

After Aspen, Misa spent a week in Downers Grove, and then we all drove to Forest Beach Camp for a week's vacation on Lake Michigan. Misa left America with a spectrum of impressions from the luxury of Aspen life, to our normal middle class life in Downers Grove, to roughing it in the cabin at the dunes.

But the best part of Misa's visit was that Jasna and Vesna got to know their uncle really well. Misa, with his great sense of humor, became their friend for life.

++

During the 1974 spring break the two Jovanovic families rented a house on Elbow Key in the Bahamas. The house came with two sunfish sailboats and several books on how to learn to sail. We all tried sailing and mostly failed. Leka, Drasko's brother, brought with him an inflatable dingy that was much greater fun for Jasna, Vesna and Dejan. Marina was fourteen months old and was not interested in either sailing or rowing. I tried to sail and was successful going one way, but could never come back. Luckily, we did all this in a shallow bay in front of the house and could push the boat back to the dock.

Drasko was the only one who fell in love with sailing. A couple of years later he bought a minifish, a 75 lb. sailboat that could fit on top of our car. Drasko loved it and sailed it on small local lakes, and off the Michigan beaches. Jasna and Vesna sailed some. I went out with Drasko a few times, but none of us really 'got it' as Drasko did.

Drasko decided that what we really should do is learn how to sail bigger sailboats. Bob Swanson, who was often at Fermilab doing experiments, was an experienced sailor. With Bob as the captain, we chartered twenty-eight to thirty-two foot sailboats several times for weekend sailing trips on the Great Lakes. We sailed out of Petoskey, Michigan; Sister Bay, Wisconsin; and Lake Side, Ohio.

Not one of these sailing trips was fully successful. We would run into storms, fog, no wind, too strong a wind, rain, no decent harbor, too many boats in the marina and no access to swimming beaches. Everything was always wet in the cabin. There was no place on the boat to lie out in the sun. On our very first trip we hit a storm on Green Bay. I was given the midnight to 4 AM shift to watch that the boat did not drag the anchor. It was windy and rainy, and I did not have fun. One day it was so foggy we could not go anywhere. We just sat in the soggy boat all day. On another trip we anchored a short distance from a nice beach. We jumped into the water to wade to the shore and walk to the beach. Instead we sunk waist deep into muck. By the time we cleaned up and got back into the boat the beach was forgotten.

Bob and Drasko loved it all. Jasna and Vesna had fun. I was not very pleased. Not to mention that to charter a boat was not a cheap affair. Drasko's big dream of the four of us sailing the Caribbean Islands was not to be. Once in a while we did rent small sailboats for short sailings. Drasko had to be satisfied with his annual minifish days at the Michigan Dunes.

Drasko did some more sailing on Lake Michigan with his friend Jim Westerman. Jim was a Chicago businessman who loved physics and via Drasko got himself involved in an experiment at Fermilab. He had a twenty-six foot sailboat in a marina in Downtown Chicago. He also had a catamaran at his summer home in Beverly Shores, Indiana. Drasko went sailing with Jim off and on for several years. Jasna, Vesna and I never did.

++

One of many international physics summer schools was held at Basko Polje on the Adriatic coast in Yugoslavia. In 1974 Drasko was invited to give a lecture there. We decided we would all go. Drasko flew directly to Split, rented a car, and drove to Basko Polje. Jasna, Vesna and I flew to Belgrade and spent a week with the family again. On the way to Split to join Drasko our flight got caught in the same airspace as the plane that carried Sri Lanka's Prime Minister Sirimavo Bandaranaike, who was on an official visit to Yugoslavia. Our plane was temporarily grounded at Zagreb airport where no one could reach us. Drasko was waiting for us at the Split airport and was told that there was no information available on our flight. For several hours there was a complete blackout on that information. Drasko nearly had a heart failure. He thought something had happened to the flight and they were not telling him. But, eventually we arrived safe and sound.

Basko Polje was a military resort with all the amenities. Drasko was not very busy, so we did lots of swimming and sightseeing. We even hiked the mountain behind the resort on a trail through olive groves. We had never been to this part of the Adriatic coast, so it was all new and very interesting to us. On the way back to Belgrade we stayed for a couple of days in Sveti Stefan, an old fishing town turned into a luxury resort, on a small island connected to the land with a short isthmus. We visited Milocer close by, the old Serbian royal family's seaside palace.

After few days in Belgrade, we flew to Amsterdam. There we visited my first cousin on my mother's side, Nikola (Nikica) Rakic, and his family whom we had never met before. Dusko and Tanja, Nikica's children, were close in age to Jasna and Vesna. They took us on a thorough sightseeing trip of Amsterdam and its vicinity. It was a very pleasant visit. A day later we were back in Downers Grove.

Right: Drasko and I soon after I arrived in Chicago. *1956*

Above: I graduated with a Master of Science in Physical Chemistry from the University of Chicago. At home at 5559 University Avenue. *1958*

Right: Drasko and I in my laboratory at the Institute for the Study of Metals on the day Drasko received his Ph.D. Chicago, *March 1960*

Paul and Estie Murphy, Drasko and I, Marija and Bogoljub (Boza) Lalevic,
Branka and Miroslav (Tosa) Todorovic, and in front, Nikola (Nidja) Nikolic, at
our first "Yugo Reunion" in Chicago. Absent were Jovan (Joca) and Anica
Jovanovic, and Vlada Skolnik. *Christmas 1956*

In the Analytical Chemistry Laboratory at the Institute for the Study of Metals at
the University of Chicago. *1957*

In the Yellowstone National Park I fed a bear sugar cubes so that Drasko could take pictures. We did not know any better then. *August 23, 1960*

Left: At Mount Rushmore on our way to California. *August 18, 1960*

Above: On the lawn of the University of California San Diego campus in La Jolla. My lab and the Pacific Ocean are in the background. *March 1961*

Left: Drasko, my father Milos Dimitrijevic, and I. Christmas in Chicago, *1962*

Left: A few days before Jasna was born on June 5, 1963. At The Point, our favorite Lake Michigan beach close to where we lived in Hyde Park, Chicago.

Right: Jasna, one month, and I, thirty-two years old. Chicago, *July 5, 1963*

Left: Jasna, in the backpack and Drasko. Westmont, Illinois. *December 12, 1963*

Right: Drasko and I three months after Jasna was born. Beverly Shores, Indiana. *August 28, 1963*

Left: Jasna, four, Vesna, ten weeks, and I, thirty-six years old. Downers Grove, Illinois, *September 4, 1967*

Right: Drasko's father Dragoljub Jovanovic, Jasna, Vesna and I. This was Cika Dragi's third and last visit to the United States. Downers Grove, Illinois. *February 1968*

Left: The first house we owned at 4808 Wallbank Ave, Downers Grove, Illinois. We lived there from 1966 until 1990. Jasna, three years old, is in front. *July 1966*

Right: An aerial view of the three cottages at the YWCA Forest Beach Camp in New Buffalo, Michigan. We vacationed there for two weeks every August from 1970 until the camp was sold in 1986.

Left: Jasna and Vesna on the dune in front of one of the three YWCA cottages. *1970*

Above: Jasna, Drasko,
Vesna, my aunt Coka
Dimitrijevic, my
nephew Dejan, Drasko's
brother Leka and his
wife Branka. This was
Coka's first visit to the
United States. *1970*

Left: My mother Emilija
Mihailovic, Vesna, Jasna
and I in our Downers
Grove front yard. This
was my mom's second
of her three visits to the
United States. *1972*

Above: My father, Milos Dimitrijevic, Vesna, Jasna, my brother Mihailo (Misa), Dejan, Aunt Coka and the family priest as he was blessing the bread on Patron Saint Archangel Michael Day-Slava. Belgrade, Yugoslavia. *November 21, 1972*

Right: Vesna, Dejan and Jasna with the suckling pig roast prepared for Slava dinner. Belgrade, Yugoslavia. *November 21, 1972*

Left: Aunt Coka, Uncle Lazar Ilijevic, I, Jasna, Vesna, Aunt Zorka (Beba) Ilijevic and my cousin Ksenija Ilijevic. Pancevo, Yugoslavia, *November 1972*

Left: Aunt Marija (Beba) Rakic, my mother's sister, Jasna, Uncle Bozidar (Bata) Rakic, Vesna, my stepfather Borislav Mihailovic and my mom. Belgrade, Yugoslavia. *July 1974*

Right: Jasna, our first dog Dandy, Drasko's mom Mira Jovanovic and Vesna. Downers Grove, Illinois. *March 1974*

Left: In an old-fashioned Serbian dress that had belonged to Drasko's grandmother, Persa Jovanovic. Downers Grove, Illinois. *1975*

Left and Below: Jasna, Drasko and I in front of Tagert Hut, at 11,250 feet in the Pearl Basin close to Aspen, Colorado. *July 1986*

Left: Our family photo taken in our Downers Grove backyard. *1978*

Left: Vesna, Jasna and I at Fontana di Trevi in Rome, Italy. We were on our way to Sicily. *1981*

Above: The view of the Grand Tetons from our house in Driggs, Idaho. Our friend Bj Bjorken's house is in the foreground on the left. *July 2004*

Left: Our house at 2646 Grand Teton Road, Driggs, Idaho. Since 1988 we have spent every summer there.

Left: Jasna, Vesna and our second dog Mickey. Batavia, Illinois. *December 1991*

Right: Jasna, in her Penn State University Ph. D. graduation gown, and Drasko, in the University of Chicago doctoral gown, at Jasna's graduation. State College, Pennsylvania. *January 1992*

Right: Leka, Vesna, Christine (Dejan's wife), Dejan, Tom Mackin (Jasna's husband), Jasna and Branka soon after Jasna and Tom moved to Champaign, Illinois.
September 1993

Left: Vesna, Jasna and their cousin Marina Jovanovic. The paintings in back, from left to right, are by my cousin Ksenija Ilijevic, by Leka Jovanovic, and by Drasko. Batavia, Illinois.
Christmas 1993

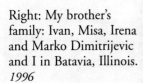

Right: My brother's family: Ivan, Misa, Irena and Marko Dimitrijevic and I in Batavia, Illinois.
1996

Right: Drasko and Î at my retirement party at Fermilab. *May 31, 1996. (Photo by Fermilab Visual Media Services.)*

Boza and Marija Lalevic, Jovan Jovanovic, Jeanie and Gene Fisk, Anica Jovanovic, Gil and Eva Clark, Branka Todorovic, Marge Hanson, Miroslav Todorovic, Nikola Sorak, I, Drasko and Katica Sorak at the Horseshoe Creek Association annual meeting. Driggs, Idaho, *August 7, 1998*

Above: Vesna and her proud parents at her graduation from the School of Medicine, University of California Davis, *June 12, 1998*

Left: Vesna, Elizabeth and Richard Lundy at Vesna's graduation. Lundys are our oldest American friends. *June 12, 1998*

Left: Jasna, Matejas, Tom and Lukas Jovanovic Mackin are the four reasons why we now live in Urbana, Illinois. *June 2002*

Left: An aerial view of our condo building on Hutchinson Island at 10680 South Ocean Drive, Jensen Beach, Florida. The arrow points to our fifth floor condo.

Right: Our home from the back yard at 213 E. Sherwin Drive, Urbana, Illinois. We have lived here since 2001.

Left: Vesna and I at Cannon Beach, Oregon, one of many beautiful places within a driving distance from Vesna's home in Portland, Oregon. *2002*

Left: Drasko and I on the Grand Targhee Ridge above Driggs, Idaho. The Grand Tetons are in the background. *2003*

Above: Leon M. Lederman Science Education Center with Fermilab in the background. *(Photo by Fermilab Visual Media Services.)*

Above: Leon M. Lederman, Marjorie G. Bardeen, Secretary of Energy Admiral James D. Watkins, I, John Peoples, Jr. and Robert R. Wilson at the Dedication Ceremony of the Science Education Center at Fermilab. At that time Peoples was Fermilab Director. Wilson and Lederman were former Fermilab directors. Marge was the Program Manager, and I was the Manager of Fermilab's Education Office. *September 25, 1992. (Photo by Fermilab Visual Media Services.)*

Dimitrijevic Family Reunion: sitting on the ground: Ivana D., Sasa D., Marko D., Mihajlo D., Jasna Jovanovic; first row: Vukica D. holding Martina D., Eta D., Zarko D., Benjamin-Beba H., Jeno-Gena H. Coka D., Ivan D., Jutka H., second row: Ildiko H. Irena D., Vera D., Olga H., Zsofia Beladi (H.), Tom Mackin, Zoltan H.; third row: Jeno-Ocsi H., Misa D., Ceda D., Bata D., Aurel H., and Drasko Jovanovic (D. = Dimitrijevic, H. = Hajto, see also the Dimiterijevic family tree on the following pages). Hungary, *May 29, 1988*

Aurel, Beba, I, Misa, Ocsi, Zsofia, Ceda and Bata, the eight Dimitrijevic cousins at the Dimitrijevic Family Reunion. Missing is Ksenija Ilijevic who was unable to attend the reunion. Hungary, *May 29, 1988*

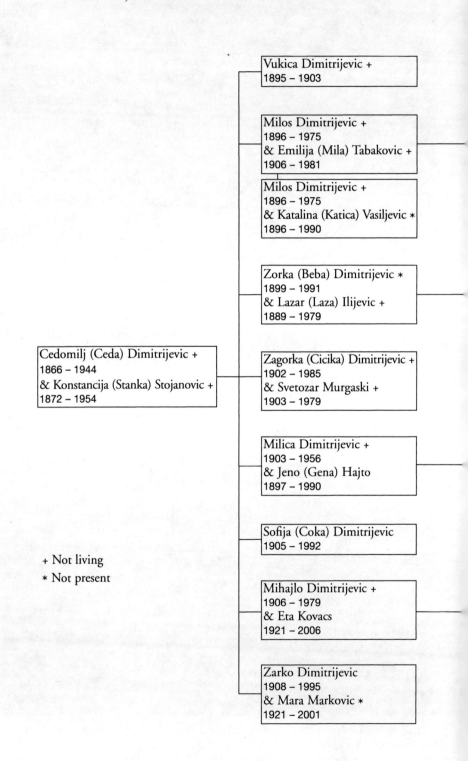

Vukica Dimitrijevic +
1895 – 1903

Milos Dimitrijevic +
1896 – 1975
& Emilija (Mila) Tabakovic +
1906 – 1981

Milos Dimitrijevic +
1896 – 1975
& Katalina (Katica) Vasiljevic *
1896 – 1990

Zorka (Beba) Dimitrijevic *
1899 – 1991
& Lazar (Laza) Ilijevic +
1889 – 1979

Cedomilj (Ceda) Dimitrijevic +
1866 – 1944
& Konstancija (Stanka) Stojanovic +
1872 – 1954

Zagorka (Cicika) Dimitrijevic +
1902 – 1985
& Svetozar Murgaski +
1903 – 1979

Milica Dimitrijevic +
1903 – 1956
& Jeno (Gena) Hajto
1897 – 1990

Sofija (Coka) Dimitrijevic
1905 – 1992

+ Not living
* Not present

Mihajlo Dimitrijevic +
1906 – 1979
& Eta Kovacs
1921 – 2006

Zarko Dimitrijevic
1908 – 1995
& Mara Markovic *
1921 – 2001

Stanka Dimitrijevic
1931
& Drasko Jovanovic
1930

Jasna Diane Jovanovic
1963
& Thomas James Mackin
1957

Vesna Ann Jovanovic *
1967

Mihailo (Misa) Dimitrijevic
1932
& Irena Sipos
1943 – 2008

Ivan Dimitrijevic
1974

Marko Dimitrijevic
1976

Ksenija Ilijevic *
1923 – 2005

Aurel Hajto
1929 – 2001
& Jutka Kolba
1937

Gabor Hajto
1963

Laszlo Hajto
1965

Zoltan Hajto
1967

Benjamin (Beba) Hajto
1930
& Olga Takacs
1942

Jeno (Ocsi) Hajto
1938
& Ildiko Kezdi-Kovacs
1942

Jan Hajto *
1968

Natali Hajto *
1969

Sofia (Zsofia) Hajto
1940 – 2005
& Miklos Beladi +
1928 – 1983

Andras (Marci) Beladi
1971

Cedomir (Ceda) Dimitrijevic
1953
& Vukica Beljanski
1953

Ivana Dimitrijevic
1979

Martina Dimitrijevic
1988

Zlatibor (Bata) Dimitrijevic
1954
& Vera Grujic
1947

Sasa Dimitrijevic
1979

Mihajlo Dimitrijevic
1980

Janet Bainbridge, a colleague, Professor Harold C. Urey and I in a lab discussion at the University of California San Diego. La Jolla, California. *1961*

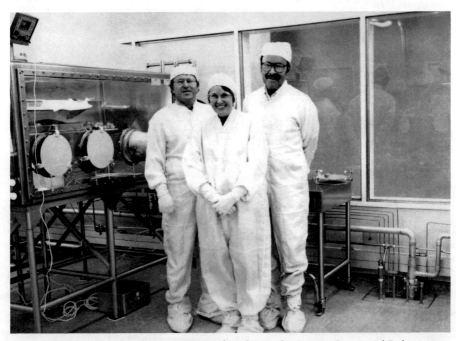

Stewart Nagle, Curator, George W. Reed and I in the Lunar Curatorial Laboratory at the Johnson Space Center. Houston, Texas. *1981*

Vlastimir (Vlasta) Vucic, Drasko's cousin and a professor of physics at the University of Belgrade, Yugoslavia, was visiting George Reed and me at the Argonne National Laboratory. George is sitting at the Nitrogen dry-box where all the lunar samples were prepared for our experiments. *March 1974*

Right: In our lab at the Brookhaven National Laboratory where George Reed and I did radiochemical analysis of many lunar samples. *1972*

The Best is yet to come! Top row: In Driggs, Idaho: Our fiftieth wedding anniversary, and Lukas and I in the hot tub. Middle row: In Urbana, Illinois: Drasko and Matejas playing chess, Lukas, Matejas and Drasko having fun at the kitchen table. Bottom row: In Urbana, Illinois: Lukas and Matejas in their backyard swimming pool, Jasna and Tom's house where we all have lots of fun. *2004*

A BIGGER HOUSE AND VESNA'S SCHOOL BAND
1975–1981

In 1975, when Jasna was twelve and Vesna was eight years old, our house became too small. Their little bedroom could not hold them both. So, we decided to look for a new house. To our surprise, houses were no longer in the twenty to thirty thousand dollar range. Our mortgage payments would have tripled just to get one more room. Albert Ramp, an architect and a contractor, and our next-door neighbor, suggested that we build an addition to our house instead. We would add two stories to the back of our Cape Cod, and gain a big bedroom upstairs, and a family room downstairs. In addition, our small upstairs bathroom would become bigger, too. To save money, Al suggested that he and Drasko do all the carpentry, dry walling, siding and painting. Al would subcontract the rest of the needed work: the foundation, masonry, roofing, electric and plumbing.

We were more than happy to follow Al's advice. The cost of the addition was estimated to be sixteen thousand dollars, which we could afford. The construction started sometime in the summer. To my amazement, all Al's sub-contractors were on the job on time. The construction schedule heavily depended on Al's and Drasko's work, and they could only work during the weekends, delaying the other contactors' work. So, instead of having the addition finished by the winter of 1975, it was completed by the spring of 1976. Al made sure the addition was enclosed and heated by the time the cold weather started, so that Drasko and he could do the interior work during the winter months. The whole project was great fun for all of us, and what was most important it stayed within the budget.

Once the addition was finished, Jasna moved into the new bedroom. Vesna stayed in their old bedroom, and our everyday life moved into the new family room. Our dining room furniture and an armchair were moved into the addition. During the day I used the dining room table as my desk, and then at five o'clock my papers would disappear and the table was set for dinner. The new family room was full of sunshine, and with the view of our pretty back yard it became a very pleasant place to be.

The whole construction project was a great learning experience for me. Everything was new to me: contracts, contractors, sub-contractors, scheduling, inspections and more. It all served me well later when I was involved in the design and construction of the Fermilab education center.

++

In 1978 the fourth school referendum failed to pass. I, of course, had never even heard the word "referendum" before, and had no clue that any local voting would affect the school budget. The failed referendum eliminated all extracurricular activities from the elementary schools in Downers Grove, including Vesna's fifth grade band.

When Vesna told me there would be no band next year, I promptly called her school principal and demanded he reinstate the band. The poor man tried to explain to me that he could not do anything about it. He suggested I go to the next School Board meeting, where the program cuts would be discussed. On the appointed day I marched to the City Hall and found it dark. The janitor who was cleaning the hallway directed me to the School Board building a few miles away. That building was also dark. Luckily, I noticed that the school building next door was fully lit with people going in. It was the right place. The meeting was in the gym. On the stage seven people sat talking among themselves. The large audience sat quietly and listened. I finally asked the person sitting next to me why nobody else was participating in the discussion. He explained that there would be a public time and that we had to wait.

The meeting started at 7 PM and finally around 11 PM the podium was opened to the public. The room exploded with complaints about program cuts, including sports, student government, yearbook and music. It was clear that the School Board could not do anything about reinstating the programs, because they were specifically voted out by the failed referendum. Finally, around 1 AM I asked if the Board would allow a parent-sponsored summer band program. The Superintendent brightened up and said that any parent-sponsored program would be considered. By the time I got home at 2 AM, I decided I was going to organize the summer band even though Vesna would not be there to participate. We were planning to spend most of the summer in Aspen, Colorado.

The next morning I called Vesna's bandleader, Mr. Schultz, who gave me the pertinent information on what it takes to run a summer band program. He assured me that if the program was organized and approved by the Superintendent, he would be more than happy to run it. I wrote a three-page proposal with the information I had, and made an appointment to see the Superintendent. He received me very politely, offered me coffee, and talked to me kindly assuming I was going to waste his time. I told him I had no time to socialize and handed the proposal to him. He took one look at it and immediately got on the phone with the bandleader, and got the Assistant Superintendent to check the legality of the undertaking I was proposing. By the time I left, there was an official summer band program in place.

But before I left, the Superintendent indicated that if I would come with a similar proposal for a parent-sponsored school year music program, he would consider it. I told him if he were serious I would expect to use the School Board facilities for meetings, including their secretarial help. I would also need to know who in town is capable, and interested in putting a proposal like that together. The Superintendent happily gave me a list of names of community leaders interested in music education. Within a few days, I had a working group of eight people I had never met before meeting in the School Board meeting room. They obviously knew how to go about creating a program that would be acceptable by the School Board, and would satisfy the Illinois School Code.

My ignorance was monumental. I did not even know that the Department of Education in Washington, DC did not rule the education system in the country. I had a hard time comprehending that the Downers Grove City Government was not in charge of the local schools. I could not believe that a bunch of citizens who got themselves elected to the School Board ruled the schools. In my frustration I went next door and asked my neighbor, Albert Ramp, to give me a brief course on how the education system in this country worked. Al did, and, in addition, gave me a copy of Roberts' Rules of Order. Luckily, I learned fast, and by the next working group meeting I was not totally uninformed.

People were so grateful that I somehow pulled them together, and provided a forum for them to work in, that they did not care how little I understood of what was going on. None of them cared that I was leaving for the summer and was not going to be able to work with them. By the time I came back in the middle of August they were meeting with the School Board lawyers to finalize the proposal for a program that the Illinois School Code would allow. It was decided that the School Board could contract a parent organization to provide the music education outside of the school day. In addition the Code allowed the students to be released into their parents' care for one hour during the school day on Wednesdays, a leftover from the old custom of releasing students into parents' care for religious education.

Within days, the Junior Music Association was organized and registered as a not-for-profit corporation in the State of Illinois. JMA and the School Board signed a contract for JMA to provide a tuition based music education, band and orchestra, in ten elementary schools and two junior high schools in Downers Grove School District #59. In turn, JMA hired a music education company out of Elkhart, Indiana to provide the music instruction. The music program had to offer scholarships for students who could not afford to pay the tuition. I called several of my friends who made tuition pledges. By the time the school year started, there were over five hundred students in the music program.

I ended up being the first JMA President. It seemed to me that I was the only one who had the guts to deal with the school system and get results. And it was worth my effort. There was no break in music education in Downers Grove school, and Vesna had her band. Five years later the political environment in Downers Grove changed and the School Board was able to absorb the music program back into the school curriculum. JMA dissolved in 1983.

In retrospect, "ignorance is bliss" applied to me. If I knew what an obstacle the outdated Illinois School Code was, how much power a school referendum had, and how afraid the people were to take the system on, I probably never would have done what I did. But Vesna wanted her band and as far as I was concerned she was going to have it no matter what. And she did.

++

In the late seventies the Downers Grove Music Club decided that the Public Library needed a new piano. Betsy Ramp, who was, I believe, the Club president at that time, was to organize a benefit concert with local talent to start raising the money. I figured it would take several concerts, and probably a few years, to raise the five thousand dollars they needed. Instead, I suggested to Betsy we invite ten of our friends, mostly members of JMA, to call ten of their friends and ask for a fifty-dollar contribution for the piano purchase. She agreed and within a week we raised enough money for the Downers Grove Library to get a new piano.

I continue to be impressed with the generosity of the people in this country. I truly believe it is only in the United States that people respond to their community needs and are willing to help, no matter how small an amount of money they can afford to give.

++

Our life in Downers Grove went on pretty normally. Jasna and Vesna were in school, Drasko was working at Fermilab, and I was working twice a week at Argonne. Branka and Leka had their own house in Wheeling, Illinois, one hour away from us. The families got together often to the children's delight. Relatives from Yugoslavia continued to come for extended visits.

Coka, my aunt came in 1970, 1976, 1981 and 1986. She loved being here and we loved having her. Coka was an easy-going, happy person full of pep. It did not bother her at all that she knew very little English. She would take off on her own to spend a day in Chicago. She walked from our Downers Grove home a mile to the railroad station, caught a train to the Union Station in Chicago, and then walked all over downtown.

Each trip was a major adventure. She would come home full of stories of what she saw and whom she talked to. She visited the museums, churches, where often somebody was playing an organ, department stores, strolled in Grant Park and along Lake Michigan, and just watched the people.

One day in 1976 she came home with a Robert Sargent Shriver, Jr. presidential campaign button. She told us "this very nice man stopped me on Michigan Avenue and we had a nice chat." She had no clue who he was or why he stopped her. She just thought that everybody in this country was nice and friendly.

Another time she stopped in a beautiful church to rest for a while. There were other people there and several stood up and told a story. So she decided she would tell them, in Serbian, about her visit with us. She did and they all applauded. She had no clue that she had been in a Christian Science Church on Wacker Drive during a testimonial time.

As a geography teacher she loved to travel. So, during one of her early visits Drasko and I gave her a present of the cheapest bus tour we could find. We did not have much money in those days and a three hundred and fifty dollar tour was pretty expensive for us. Coka spent a week traveling through Missouri and the Lakes of the Ozarks and had a grand time.

But the best part was that being with Coka for months at a time Jasna and Vesna learned Serbian. Coka spoke only Serbian with them and they understood each other perfectly. Coka spoke

German, Hungarian and Serbian, and she saw no need to learn English, too. She knew enough to get around and that was all she cared about.

We all loved Coka and were very sad when she passed away on September 27, 1992. She was eighty-seven.

++

My mom visited three times: in 1965, 1972 and in 1977. Her last visit was after my stepfather, Bora Mihailovic, died on June 9, 1977. In 1978 Vesna and I went to visit her in Belgrade. Without Cika Bora my mom did not do well on her own. It was not an easy visit for me. I found a good woman to look after her but my mom could not stand to have a live-in person, and pretty soon my brother Misa had to move her in with his family. I went to Belgrade again in 1980 to find a nursing home for her. Misa just could not deal with that. I found a nice home run by Catholic nuns in Zrenjanin, a town a couple of hours away from Belgrade. Misa and Irena struggled to keep Mom at home as long as they could. Finally they had to put her into the nursing home, where she died a few months later on February 3, 1981. She was seventy-five years old.

Drasko's dad visited in 1958, then both Cika Dragi and Teta Mira came together in 1964. Cika Dragi came again alone in 1968. He died on February 19, 1970. He was seventy-nine years old. Teta Mira came again in 1973 and 1976. She died in June 1982. She was also seventy-nine.

In July 1975 I went to Belgrade to visit my father who was in the hospital with lung cancer. All his life he had been a heavy smoker. He died two month later on October 11, 1975. He was seventy-nine. He visited us only once in 1962.

Misa and Irena married soon after our father died, and moved in with our stepmother, Tetka Katica. From then on when in Belgrade we stayed with them. I was there again in 1979, 1980, 1981 and 1983. My last visit to Belgrade was in 1988 when I was on the way to Hungary for the Dimitrijevic family reunion organized by my cousin Aurel Hajto.

Jasna is the only one of us who has spent a longer time in Belgrade. She spent the 1987–1988 school year in Belgrade doing research for her doctoral dissertation on a Fulbright-Hays Fellowship. She stayed with Misa's family. In 1990 she spent another six months there to complete her research.

Vesna has visited in Yugoslavia several times. Her last visit was in February 1988, when she went to visit Jasna.

++

We continued to go to the sea during the school spring breaks. In 1979 we were in Negril, Jamaica, where we had an unpleasant experience. We stayed in a resort complex of several villas. Late one night four young native men came to the resort with machetes, attacked the night guard, and abducted two American women from the villa a couple of doors away from us. The husbands were there, but there was nothing they could do without getting killed. The police were called, and a search was mounted. Two hours later the women, who had been raped in sugar cane fields, returned. The next day, the police arrested the perpetrators, but we all doubted that any justice would be done.

The sad part was that the husband of one of the women was a doctor who was in Jamaica considering possibly relocating his practice there. After that experience I am sure he did not move. The good thing that came out of the event was that we befriended a German family in the villa next to us. Kurt, a Lufthansa flight engineer, Brunhield his wife and their son Mirko Wiedemann were on spring break, too. Together we tried to find a more protected hotel to move to. But the hotels we looked at were so walled in that you had to go in search to find the beach.

Instead, we decided for our two families to move into one villa, board the doors and windows, and spend the rest of the vacation where we were. Those several days of togetherness, that reminded me of our refugee days during WWII, made our two families friends for life. In the coming years we visited them several times in Germany, and they came to visit us, too. In 2001, Vesna visited

Mirko in Munich, Germany, and Bruni and Kurt in Mas Sant Miguel, in the South of France, where they had retired. Kurt and Bruni came to Jasna and Tom's wedding in June 1992. That was the last time we saw them in the United States.

SICILY, FRIENDS OF FERMILAB, IDAHO
AND FAMILY REUNION
1981–1989

Antonio Zichichi was an Italian high-energy physicist at CERN, European Center for Nuclear Physics. When in 1980 Zichichi announced he was coming to visit Fermilab, Leon M. Lederman, Fermilab Director, asked Drasko, who was then the head of the Fermilab Physics Department, to be Zichichi's host.

As part of Zichichi's activities we had him and his wife Mima (Maria Ludovica Bernardini) for dinner at our house. The Zichichis turned out to be very pleasant and charming people. Jasna and Vesna, who usually escaped to their rooms when we had company, stayed with us throughout the evening. Sandra and Brad Cox (also a Fermilab physicist) were the only other dinner guests the Zichichis had asked us to invite. So the group was small and the conversation lively.

A year later in 1981, Zichichi invited Drasko to be one of the lecturers at the Summer School for High-Energy Physics at the Ettore Majorana Centre in Erice in Sicily in Italy. He invited all four of us to come to Erice with all expenses paid. To this day I am convinced that our dinner party "paid off."

We got the royal treatment. In Naples we walked into a designated travel agency and received a package of information for our trip to Erice. We boarded a high-speed hydrofoil ferryboat that took us to Palermo. We were met at the dock by a liveried chauffeur who escorted us to a black limousine. In a couple of hours, very late at night, we arrived at the heavy door of an ancient monastery. The gatekeeper escorted us to our quarters in the old church tower. The tower was Zichichi's private four-level apartment assigned to us. The living room was on the top level, then two levels of a bedroom each, and the bathroom on the bottom level. When we woke up the next morning an overwhelming view of the west end of Sicily, of the Mediterranean Sea and of the roofs of Erice was all around us. The medieval town of Erice was on a hill two thousand feet above the sea and the town of Tripani.

In addition, outside of our bedroom there was a long terrace just below the roofline of the old church. Along the terrace there were openings where you could see the old church ceiling covered with frescos. The church and the rest of the cloister were remodeled to provide the conference facilities and several apartments for VIP guests. We found ourselves in the company of Paul Dirac, Edward Teller, Eugene Wigner, Val Fitch, Shelly Glashow and Karl Berkelman and their families. All but Teller, Berkelman and Drasko had Nobel Prizes. If it was not for the dinner party we hosted for Zichichi in Downers Grove we would never had had the opportunity to even breathe the same air with so many famous people at the same time. At least I believed so.

We ate breakfast together at the cloister, had boxed lunches when we wanted to go to the beach, and free access to all the restaurants in Erice for all other meals. The Zichichi's son, a handsome young man, drove Jasna, Vesna and me in his jeep nearly every day to the best beach in the area. Joan Glashow and Mary Berkelman had their own rented cars. There were four Glashow children, three boys and a little girl, and three Berkelman boys, teens and pre-teens, who came to the beach too. Jasna and Vesna and the other young people became friends and did lots of things together.

One day all the lecturers came to the beach for a day of swimming and a dinner at a beach restaurant. We all discovered that Edward Teller was missing a foot. He calmly told us the story that when he was a young boy a tramway car rode over his foot and that's how he lost it. He was perfectly happy hopping around on the stump while the rest of us tried not to stare.

There were two major social events organized by the Centre. One was a banquet, and the other a trip to tour Greek temples. The banquet was an evening affair in the courtyard of the restored Governor's

Palace. The catacombs, accessible from the courtyard, had tables laid out with a variety of foods. I still remember the room with desserts where one long table was covered with a variety of marzipan and almond cakes in all shapes and forms. Marzipan was, and still is, one of my favorite desserts. Marzipan was a local food staple available everywhere in Erice. But the display at the banquet was something to be remembered. Several folklore groups entertained us. Dancing came later. Paul Dirac was an eighty-two year old gentleman who just sat and watched everybody else dance. At one point I asked him if he would like to dance and he said yes. So he and I danced, and I believe he enjoyed it very much.

The busses took the lecturers, their families and the Summer School students (also physicists) on a day trip to see the Greek temples at Segesta and Selinunte. Close to Selinunte we had lunch at a beach restaurant. After lunch Paul Dirac decided to go for a swim. Zichichi asked a student to go with Dirac. After a long swim they came out of the water stung all over by multitudes of Portuguese man-of-war jellyfish. It did not bother Dirac, but the poor student was miserable.

After the Summer School was over we spent a day touring Palermo. Then we boarded the hydrofoil back to Naples. From Naples we took the train to Rome, and from Rome we flew back to Chicago.

Many years later Ellen Lederman, an art photographer, had an exhibit at Fermilab. Among her photographs were several from Erice and Selinunte. Drasko and I bought her photo of *Acropolis at Selinunte*. Later Ellen gave us *Roofs of Erice* as a present. Both photos now hang in our house in Urbana. They evoke the wonderful memories we have of our summer in Erice.

++

On the way to Erice, Jasna, Vesna and I flew to Belgrade to visit the family. While there, Jasna realized that her grandmother Mira, Drasko's mom, was unhappy because she and Vesna had never been christened. To make her grandma Baka Mira happy Jasna decided she was going to be christened. Jasna felt strongly enough about it that

Misa, my brother, and I decided to have both his children and mine christened at the same time.

Misa and I went to our Eastern Orthodox Archdiocese (Patrijarsija) to make special arrangements because Jasna and Vesna were not Yugoslav citizens. The priest we talked to was very accommodating and the date was set for the christening. As we were leaving we ran into an old friend, Mile Carnic, a theology professor. We exchanged greetings, and I thought nothing of it. Unfortunately, the priest, who was still with us, decided to please me by using the christening rite recently translated from an ancient church text by Professor Carnic. What that meant was that the simple christening rite that the priest used to christen Jasna and Vesna, with Misa as the Godfather, lasted ten minutes. The ancient rite used to christen Misa's sons, Ivan and Marko, with me as their Godmother, lasted over half an hour. Standing still, with two wiggly young boys, nearly killed me. So much for knowing famous people.

The christening was performed in Saborna Crkva, our main Eastern Orthodox Church in Belgrade. Many family members were present, including a very happy, weeping Baka Mira. At the time Jasna was eighteen, Vesna was fourteen, Ivan was seven and Marko was five years old.

++

After two weeks in Belgrade we were on our way to Rome to meet Drasko. We took a train from Belgrade to Kranjska Gora in Slovenia. I had spent many vacations in Kranjska Gora before I left for America. My aunt Coka came along with us, and she and I had a great time showing Jasna and Vesna our favorite places and the mountain trails we had hiked many years ago.

Coka said goodbye to us in Jasenice where we caught a night train to Villach, Austria. In Villach we were to catch the train to Rome. We arrived in Villach at one in the morning and within minutes we were the only people left in the railroad station. I was at a total loss. There was nobody anywhere I could ask what to do. Luckily, several minutes later our train engineer walked through the station, saw us, and asked why we were still there. It turned out that we were not at the main Villach railroad station . The one we were at was just for local travel. The man offered to drive us to the main station, and we gratefully accepted.

Jasna, Vesna and I arrived in Rome before Drasko. We checked into our hotel and became professional tourists. Two days later we waited on a corner, outside the Rome railway station, for the airport bus to bring Drasko. It all worked out as planned, and we had a great week touring Rome. I calculated that I had walked seventy miles in seven days, which brought about a bursitis in my right hip that took five years to heal. But the cultural fun we had was monumental.

From Rome we went to Naples by train. We spent a day touring Naples, and a day on Capri Island. On the third day we were on our way to Erice.

++

In April 1981, Drasko asked me to tell Leon M. Lederman, then Fermilab Director, how to organize "friends" to raise private funds to enable Fermilab to offer programs to high school science teachers. Apparently science teachers were coming to Fermilab's Saturday Morning Physics, a series of lectures for high school students, to learn with the students. That told Leon that teachers also needed to learn modern physics. Fermilab had all the resources to help, but could not use federal funds to do so.

Based on my experience with the Junior Music Association I wrote a talking paper and went to Fermilab and handed it to Leon. Leon's reaction was: "all I need is a two million dollar endowment enough for Fermilab to have programs for science teachers." I wished him good luck and went home.

But Leon started me thinking. So, I picked up the phone and called Robert McCullough, a business executive who lived in Geneva, Illinois. I asked him how easy it would be to raise two million dollars. I expected Bob to laugh me off. Instead, he said: "it depends what you need it for." I knew Bob was an experienced fundraiser, and to my surprise, he thought that in spite of Fermilab being a federally funded institution funds could be raised for science education programs.

Several months later on February 2, 1982, after a pleasant dinner party, Drasko and I were saying good night to Leon on his doorstep. It was a bitterly cold night. Suddenly, standing in the freezing cold Leon asked me to please do something about creating Friends of Fermilab. The man is really serious, I thought. A few days later I decided to ask Marjorie G. Bardeen, president of a local school board, if she would be willing to help. Marge thought for a moment, and said yes, but only if teachers have the say in what kind of programs Fermilab would offer. Then I called Bob McCullough and he agreed to help. I asked Jeanie Fisk, who ran her own preschool in Batavia, if she would help. She thought it was a good idea for Fermilab to do something to help schools teach science. Ellen Lederman had no choice but to help. So, I went to Leon with my conditions: we would work out of his office and his assistant Judy Zielinski would help. Leon agreed, and the organizing group was born.

Bob McCullough's friends Carl Safanda, a lawyer, and Malcolm Douglas, an accountant and a financial advisor, joined the group a few months later. They were both essential in helping us sort out all the legalities on how to create and run an organization. Officially, Fermilab staff could not give any legal or accounting advice to an outside group, even though everybody at Fermilab was eager to see Friends become a reality.

Between March and May 1982, the group met several times and developed a proposal to organize Friends of Fermilab Association. Late in May 1982, the proposal was presented to Leon, who promptly presented it to Fermilab's Board of Trustees. On October 3, 1982 I was summoned to come to Fermilab to talk to the Trustees. They whole-heartedly approved of the Friends, but were very skeptical about our ability to raise money for Fermilab, an institution funded by taxpayer's money.

I did not get discouraged. I spent that summer reading books on foundations and how to raise private funds. I was pretty sure the funds could be raised for science education regardless of Fermilab being a federal institution. As far as I was concerned, just making Fermilab scientists available to local schools was something any foundation official should be more than willing to fund. And I was more or less right.

After the Trustees approved the proposed organization, Marge Bardeen, with the help of Marguerite (Marge) Cox, George Zahrobsky and William (Bill) West, educators from area schools, orchestrated a needs assessment with educators and community leaders to identify how best Fermilab could help science education in local schools. The outcome was the proposal for the *Summer Institute for Science Teachers.*

FFLA was incorporated on March 8, 1983 as an Illinois not-for-profit corporation. Three days later we mailed our very first grant proposal to forty foundations and to the Department of Energy. On March 13, 1983, the *A Nation at Risk* report was published bemoaning the country's state of science education. On March 16, 1983 FFLA received enough money from three foundations and the Department of Energy to run its very first program: *Summer Institute for Science Teachers.* Our timing could not have been better.

The 1983 Summer Institute was the first program FFLA offered at Fermilab. Many more followed, including the construction of the Leon M. Lederman Science Education Center. Thousands of teachers and several hundred thousands of students from across the country have participated in over thirty Fermilab programs. The Education Center is the crowning glory of the effort started by our small organizing group. In retrospect, I can hardly believe we had the guts to do it. But we did it, and I am certainly proud to have been a part in making it all possible.

I was FFLA's president for 13 years. In 1989 I became the Manager of the newly created Fermilab Education Office. Marge Bardeen became its Program Manager. After I retired in 1996, Marge took over both jobs, that of FFLA President and of Education

Office Manager. Under her direction both organizations are doing great.

++

After *A Nation at Risk* was published in 1983 it was said that President Reagan asked his cabinet members to find a way to support science education through their Departments. Richard Stevens was in charge of college education programs in the Office of Energy Research at the Department of Energy. His Office co-funded the 1983 *Summer Institute for Science Teachers* at Fermilab. As soon as it was obvious that the Summer Institute was a major success Rich invited me to share Fermilab's story with the education officers from other DOE national laboratories at their annual meeting in San Juan, Puerto Rico. I went, and to my disappointment the organizers would not give me time to make my presentation. They managed programs for college students and had no interest in pre-college programs. The benefit for me was that I got to know these people and I learned how they operate.

At the next annual meeting Rich Stevens made sure that both Marge Bardeen and I were present. We outlined Fermilab's pre-college science education organization and program development process. Soon after, funding became available from DOE, and many of the national labs initiated their own pre-college science education programs. At the peak there were 387 programs offered at 25 facilities. Over 159,000 teachers and over 750,000 students participated in these programs in 1994. Today, in 2004, the number of facilities offering programs remains about the same, but only 23,771 teachers and 383,710 students participated in 229 programs.

Fermilab's Leon M. Lederman Science Education Center continues to offer a full slate of programs. From the very beginning in 1982, Marge developed a needs assessment process to design programs working with area educators and Fermilab scientists. In this way the programs reflected current needs of teachers and their students. To this day all the programs offered at Fermilab are well attended. In addition, a teacher resource center was developed that today is one of the Nation's best multimedia library for K-12 science teachers. The Center also had, and still has, hands-on physics exhibits opened to the public and schools.

Major credit goes to Leon for his foresight to open Fermilab to the K-12 school community. But it was Marge Bardeen, her staff and I that made it possible for Fermilab to become a major national resource to science teachers. To this day I claim that the only reason Admiral James D. Watkins, then Secretary of Energy, came to Fermilab twice during his tenure was for the Education Center groundbreaking and then to the dedication ceremonies.

During my tenure as Friends of Fermilab President and Fermilab's Education Office Manager I participated in many conferences, workshops and other meetings dealing with pre-college science education. They were held all over the country, some in very nice places like Santa Fe, New Orleans, Palo Alto, Atlanta and Washington, DC. We even helped organize programs for physics teachers in Mexico City, Mexico. That took Drasko and me, and other education staff, for a visit to Mexico City. Many of these places I would have never seen since I had no reason to go there.

++

Jane Wilson, wife of Robert R. Wilson, founding Director of Fermilab, was a financial wizard. She believed that very few physicists and their wives knew much about family finance. So, when a large number of physicists and their spouses were in Snowmass, Colorado, at the 1982 Future of High-Energy Physics Workshop, Jane asked Judith Garelick, another spouse who was also a financial adviser from Boston, Massachusetts, to educate the rest of us on family finances. Jane invited us all for coffee and had Judith make a presentation to us. I could not believe half of what I heard that day. There would not be a government pension when we retired. We had to save and to manage our own retirement fund, and one should invest the savings and not keep the funds in a checking account. Judith showed us how to analyze and plan our family finances. Most all of it was news to me.

Judith offered to do a financial analysis for free for anyone present. I signed up, and with her advice I ended up investing into an IRA, a term life insurance and a savings certificate. Once back home in Downers Grove I promptly signed up for a College of DuPage extension course in family finance held at Downers Grove North High School. I also attended a seminar on income tax at the Downers Grove Library. A few days later I hired Charles Zapotocky, who was one of the seminar speakers, to do our income tax returns and he has been doing them ever since.

I was fifty-one years old when I learned how one is supposed to take care of the financial health of one's family. I told Drasko I was taking over the management of our finances. Drasko could not be happier. It was a burden he had no interest in. The ultimate result was that by the time we retired in the mid-nineties we had enough money to live comfortably. Thanks to the stock market boom in the 1990s, we also had enough money to finance both Tom and Jasna's, and Vesna's homes. We were able to help Tom and Jasna buy their lake cottage. We bought Vesna a new car when she graduated from medical school. We also had enough money to afford to buy our condo on Hutchinson Island in Florida.

And all of this was thanks to Jane Wilson and her concerns for the financial well being of the physicists' families.

++

In late September 1987, Drasko and I were in Salt Lake City, Utah, where Drasko gave an invited talk at the National Science Teachers Association annual meeting. After the meeting we rented a car and drove to Driggs, Idaho, on our way to Jackson, Wyoming. Drasko saw the Teton Valley, where Driggs is located, from the Grand Teton when he climbed it in 1984. He wanted to take photos of the west side of the Grand Teton, the side he climbed. We were going to stay overnight at the Grand Targhee Ski Resort, so that Drasko could take his time and find the best place to take photos. Unfortunately, the resort just acquired a new owner and it was closed for remodeling.

Once back down in the Valley we notice several "lots for sale" signs. We could not see any lots, only fields of alfalfa, barley and such. I wanted more information, so we stopped at one of the two realtors in town. Tom Knight, a laidback, happy-looking person immediately insisted on driving us around and showing us the lots available for sale. Tom drove us through the fields on bumpy roads, and gave us several sheets of plats to ponder over.

That night we stayed in Driggs in the Best Western motel, the only one in town. The next morning we drove over the Teton Pass to Jackson. We stayed in Jackson for a couple of nights. It was early October and the weather was sunny and clear. During the day it was in the seventies, and at night in the thirties. The aspens were golden yellow, the oaks were red and the evergreens were green. The Tetons were peppered with fresh snow. The scenery was breathtaking. We did a few hikes in Grand Teton National Park, and altogether had a great time. The best part was it was late in the season, and there were very few tourists around.

On the way back to Salt Lake City we stopped in Driggs again for Drasko to take more photos of the Grand Teton. While driving through the beautiful and peaceful Teton Valley with the Tetons hovering above, I told Drasko we were going to buy a piece of land with a view of the Tetons even if we never came back again. Drasko agreed and we stopped by to look at lots in Teewinot subdivision. The subdivision was located straight west of the Grand Teton range, and the view of the three Teton peaks was magnificent.

We looked at one-acre lots priced at five thousand dollars that we could afford. While we were looking at one of the lots, we realized that a small house nearby was also for sale. We walked over and peaked through a window. We saw a fully equipped kitchen and a carpeted living room. The house was obviously livable. It sat on 2.7 acres of land, and it was listed at thirty-six thousand dollars. Compared to prices in Aspen, Colorado, where I was looking at properties earlier that summer, this was dirt-cheap. I tried to telephone Tom Knight to ask him to show us the house. It was Sunday and he was nowhere to be found. Drasko and I decided to make an offer for the house without seeing it inside. Later that evening we called Tom from Pocatello, Idaho and made an offer for the house. Several months later we became the owners of the eight hundred square foot house we had never seen inside. We also ended up paying forty thousand dollars for it, more than its listed price. Apparently, the information we had was a couple of years old.

A bit of history: the house was built by Mr. Floyd Bagley, the father-in-law of John A. McKellar, a well-known realtor in Driggs and the President of the LDS Stake in the Valley. In 1971, when the Grand Targhee ski hill was opened for day skiing, Mr. Bagley subdivided two hundred forty acres of his land on Hastings Lane, two miles north of Driggs. Teewinot was one of the early subdivisions in the Valley. Then he built four small houses at the south west corner of the land for his wife and his three daughters. The house we bought was Mrs. Vivian Bagley's house. She lived there until she passed away in 1985.

I should mention that we were able to buy the house because Drasko's parents' apartment in Belgrade was sold sometime earlier that year. We used part of that money as the down payment for the Driggs house.

++

I furnished the house in Driggs over the phone. The furniture store in Driggs sent me pictures of the furniture they carried to select from. I did, and when we arrived in July 1988, a couch, a small dining room table and six chairs, and the beds were already delivered and placed in the house by the storeowner. We quickly found out how people live in a small community like Driggs. Everybody knew and trusted each other. A handshake was a valid contract. The plumber would come to the house, and if nothing was wrong, or just a small adjustment was to be made, there was no charge. If you had a flat tire you called the local mechanic who came to the house, picked up the tire, repaired it and brought it back for very little money. Friendly local people prevailed everywhere.

In 1991 we decided to build an addition to the house. We needed more room for ourselves and for the many guests who came to visit. Our friends, who would not bother to come to Illinois, were happy to come and visit us in Driggs. We loved having them. There was much to do and see within driving distance, and nobody needed to be entertained. Grand Teton National Park and Jackson were an hour away. Yellowstone National Park was an hour and a half away. Many hiking trails were easily accessible. The weather was perfect all the time. In the summer the temperature was in the eighties and nineties during the day, and in the fifties to sixties at night. It rarely rained.

We hired a contractor, who spelled out to the last nail what he would do for us. The construction started in the fall of 1991. I went to Driggs twice during that winter to see how the work was progressing. By April 1992 the addition was finished. We had nearly doubled the size of the house with a new master bedroom and a bath, a living room, a laundry room and a coat closet. In the process we had remodeled the old kitchen, and added a dishwasher. We got a new metal roof and an outdoor hot tub. In time, our old upright piano arrived in Driggs to Drasko's and Vesna's delight. Altogether, our standard of living vastly improved.

Jasna and her family, and Vesna, loved coming to Driggs. Over time many of their friends also came to visit The young people did many hikes and backpacking trips. Swimming in Jackson Lake was another favorite activity. Just sightseeing the gorgeous country was a treat.

Since we retired in 1997, Drasko and I have spent summers in Driggs. We hike, sit in the hot tub, or just sit on the deck and stare at the Tetons. During the winter ski season the house is rented once in a while, but we never go there then. Skiing has never been our favorite sport.

++

In 1989, I got together a group of our old friends to buy one hundred and thirty acres of land on the west side of the Teton Valley. Under my supervision the land was subdivided into twenty-four five-acre lots and a six-acre park. We then built the road and brought electric service to each lot. The land came with shares of water rights that made it possible to have the land irrigated and farmed. The water was diverted from Horseshoe Creek into a big pond in our park. From the pond an underground irrigation system we installed brought the water to each lot. We also had the electric company bury the cables along the east perimeter of the property that were spoiling the view of the Grand Tetons. We built a picnic shelter in the park, and built an imposing log archway at the entrance. We called the subdivision Horseshoe Creek Ranch, a very nice place to be.

The Horseshoe Creek group included our Yugoslav friends, the Jovanovics, the Lalevics, the Todorovics and the Soraks, and our good friends Marge and Bill Bardeen, Gil and Eva Clark, Marge Hanson, Leon and Ellen Lederman, Gene and Jeanie Fisk, Janine and Alvin Tollestrup and George Reed. We all had plans to retire there, but it did not work out that way. Only the Hansons built a house. Some lots got sold, and two more houses were built. The rest of the land is just sitting and waiting for the next generation to enjoy. The good news is that as of 2004, the value of our original investment has grown by a factor of seven.

Several of our friends bought property in Teton Valley. Leon and Ellen Lederman, James (BJ) Bjorken, Sandy and David Anderson, Marge Hanson and her family and Janine and Alvin Tollestrup have built or bought houses in the Valley. Nearly thirty of our friends now own property in the Teton Valley. I like to think it was all thanks to Drasko and me, and our foresight in buying the house in the Teton Valley.

++

My cousin Aurel Hajto was two years older than me. He was the oldest son of my father's younger sister Milica. She was married to Jeno Hajto, the son of my grandmother Stanka's best friend. Milica and Jeno (Gena) and their four children lived in Budapest, Hungary.

Aurel called me early in 1988 to ask if my family and I would come to Hungary if he organized a Dimitrijevic family reunion there. I loved the idea, especially since I had last seen him and his family in 1942.

Thanks to Aurel's dedicated effort, thirty-one of thirty-eight Ceda and Stanka Dimitrijevic descendants and their spouses, gathered in May 1988 for a three-day family celebration. Aurel was the Commercial Director at the Computing and Management Organization Company. The company owned a country estate, Berzsenyi Kastely in Somjenmihalyfa in Hungary, used for conferences and retreats. The beautiful mansion had plenty of room for all of us, including several social and game rooms and very nice grounds. There was also a kitchen staff with an excellent cook. For three days we lived in a splendor very few of us had experienced before.

In one of the rooms we created a display of old family documents and photos going back to the mid-nineteenth century. We learned a lot about ancestors many of us did not even know existed. Several of the documents were ones I had brought with me from my aunt Zorka (Beba) from Pancevo in Yugoslavia. She was too old and feeble to travel. I still have them, and someday I plan to compile them in a booklet for the rest of the family to have. Aurel had a tape recording set up for us and many recorded their thoughts about the family history. I have the tapes, and have yet to listen to any of them.

Three generations were present. Aunt Coka, Uncle Zarko, Aunt Eta and Uncle Jeno were the generation before me. Everybody from my generation was there, except Ksenija who stayed home to look after Aunt Beba. Fifteen cousins and their spouses aged thirty-four to fifty-nine where together for the very first time. Several had never met before. There were twelve present from the third generation; missing was my daughter Vesna, and Ocsi Hajtos's children, Jan and Natali.

The pleasant meals, walks through the grounds, playing with children, talking in small and large groups and just catching up and getting to know each other again were the main activities of the day. The main event of the reunion celebration was a dinner with speeches, toasts and a big cake.

The parting was very sentimental. We promised each other we would get together again every few years. We tried, but the Balkan war in the nineteen-nineties prevented it.

One immediate fun thing that came out of the reunion was that Zoltan, Aurel's youngest son who was twenty-five at the time, came to visit us later that summer. He came with us to Driggs, then to the Cape May Point, where we had a "Yugo" reunion, and then to the Michigan Dunes. He, Jasna and Vesna got to know each other well, and to this day Zoltan is our main link to our family in Budapest.

Aurel and Jutka, his wife, visited us in Downers Grove in 1990. After that time I have never seen him again. The good feeling I have is that Vesna visited Aurel and his family three weeks before he passed away in September 2001. Somehow I felt like I was there, too.

TWICE RETIRED
1989–2004

George Reed, my colleague at Argonne National laboratory, was sixty-nine years old in 1989 when he decided to retire. That gave me a good reason to retire, too. I was ready to dedicate my time to the construction of the Fermilab education center, and to leave my life as a research scientist behind. I was fifty-eight years old when I left Argonne in May 1989.

In September 1989 Fermilab decided to create an education office to supervise the construction of the education center. I was hired as the Education Office Manager and my friend Marge Bardeen was the Education Office Program Manager. Many of the pre-college science programs sponsored by Friends of Fermilab were already well established and running. The big project was to design hands-on physics exhibits that teachers and students, and the walk-in public, would use at the Center. A multimedia resource library, a computer room and a life science laboratory were also developed and constructed.

The groundbreaking ceremony for the Center was on October 7, 1989. The dedication ceremony was on September 25, 1992, with ribbon cutting and many speeches. Among the dignitaries present at both events were Admiral James D. Watkins, the Secretary of Energy, and State Representative J. Dennis Hastert, the current Speaker of the House. Robert R. Wilson and Leon M. Lederman, past Fermilab Directors, and John Peoples, Jr., then Fermilab Director, were also present.

By the time I retired from Fermilab in 1996, the Leon M. Lederman Science Education Center and its programs were well known both locally and across the country.

+-+

After I left Argonne, Drasko and I decided to move closer to

Fermilab. We were now both working there and there was no reason why we should not live close to Fermilab. So, in June 1990 we bought a house in Batavia, less than a mile from Fermilab. The house at 615 Viking Drive was three years old, with four bedrooms, a study, dining room, a big kitchen, a big living room, a deck and an attached two-car garage. Not to mention a two-person Jacuzzi bath in the master bathroom. After living in our Downers Grove Cape Cod house for twenty-four years, we found that living in a new, modern house was heaven.

The best part was that we had plenty of room for all the Jovanovics to stay comfortably for several days during the Christmas holidays, including Jasna's, Dejan's and Marina's future spouses Thomas Mackin, Christine Schaak and Keir Davis. These were fun occasions for all of us.

++

In 1991 both Jasna and Vesna were living in Santa Barbara, California. Jasna and Tom were post-docs at the University of California Santa Barbara. They had a very nice apartment, on a beautiful golf course, with plenty of room for us to stay. Vesna was working for *Islands* magazine, and had her own apartment. A year later Vesna decided to go back to school at Santa Barbara City College in preparation for applying to medical schools.

Drasko's and my visits to Santa Barbara were great adventures. The weather was always sunny and pleasant. Everything was in perpetual bloom. The Pacific Ocean was beautiful, and our children were happy. Vesna stayed in Santa Barbara until 1994, when she moved to Davis to attend the UC Davis Medical School.

Jasna and Tom were married in 1992 and then moved to Urbana, Illinois in 1993. They both became assistant professors at the University of Illinois Urbana-Champaign. Urbana was one hundred thirty-five miles south from Batavia, an easy driving distance from us.

Vesna stayed in California until 1998, and then moved to Vancouver, Washington for her residency program. She now lives in

Portland, Oregon, where she is a family physician.

++

It was apparent that after Drasko retired there was no reason why we should not move closer to Jasna and Tom. They were planning to provide us with grandchildren in the near future. So, in November 1996 we bought a brand new house in Champaign, in the Ponds of Windsor subdivision, two miles from Jasna and Tom. Drasko was invited to teach at the University of Illinois, which he happily did. In 1997 and in 1998 he taught a course during the spring semester. In November 1997 he fully retired from Fermilab, and in early 1998 we moved permanently to Champaign. Once there Drasko taught a course during the fall semesters, so we could spend the winter months in Florida.

Our first grandchild, Matejas Walter Jovanovic Mackin was born on May 6, 1998. Drasko and I were deliriously happy. We insisted on taking care of him while Jasna and Tom were at work. We happily baby-sat until Matko (I call him Matko, Drasko calls him Mateja and everybody else calls him Tej) became too heavy and too active for us to handle. Jasna then found Mary Arriola, a wonderful woman much younger than us, to look after Matko full time. We were sad, but at the same time relieved not to have the responsibility of taking care of a small, very active child.

Two years later, Lukas Milos (Milos was my father's name) Jovanovic Mackin was born on June 12, 2000. Soon after, Jasna decided we should live much closer to them so that we could walk to each other's homes. In October 2001 we moved to our present house at 213 E. Sherwin Drive in Urbana, two blocks from Jasna and Tom's house.

When we are at home in Urbana, and not in Florida, Oregon or Idaho, we see Matko and Lule (I call him Lule, everybody else calls him Luki) every day. Last fall, 2003, they were five and three years old, grown up enough to walk from their house to our house on their own. We did watch them from both homes as they walked, but still they were proud they could come to visit us on their own. We went over to their house every day to play with the kids. They all came to visit us very often. The best fun I had with Matko and Lule was when we played in their swimming pool. We dove for treasures, we raced across the shallow end of the pool, and they would jump into the pool over and over again. I remembered I played with Jasna and Vesna the same way when they were at that age. Often Jasna would make dinner, and we would eat out on the deck in their backyard surrounded by a prairie park and a small forest.

++

The nineteen-ninetieth tragic war in the Balkans did upset many people's lives in Yugoslavia. Misa, my brother, was worried that his two sons, Ivan 17 and Marko 15 years old in 1991, could end up fighting in the war nobody wanted. So in 1992, Ivan came to California as a high school senior on an exchange program. A year later he became an electrical engineering student at Northern Illinois University in De Kalb, Illinois. Two years later Marko also came, and became a computer science student at NIU. The boys were very industrious and both graduated with Master degrees in their respective fields, Ivan in 1998 and Marko in 2000. Today they are gainfully employed, Ivan in New Jersey, and Marko in California.

Misa and Irena, my sister-in-law, stayed in Yugoslavia. Life without their boys must have been, and must still be very lonely. Marko, a very able young man, was diligently sending his family members' names to the United States Immigration Lottery program, and, to everybody's pleasant surprise, Misa and Irena received green cards in 1997. That made it easy for them to travel to the United States and visit Ivan and Marko as often as they could. When they are here we make a point of seeing them, too.

++

We bought our Florida condo in 1994. In the late nineteen-eighties, Drasko and I realized that as we got older vacationing in the Caribbean Islands would become harder for us. Few islands had decent supermarkets or medical services, which would become

185

more and more important to us. The islands that had all we needed, such as the American Virgin Islands or Grand Cayman, were over-developed and too expensive. We decided that Florida was the place where we should own a condominium and spend winter months once we retired.

So every time we vacationed in Florida we looked at condos to buy. I spent time with realtors on Longboat Key, in Venice, in Englewood Beach and on Don Pedro Island. These were areas on the Gulf Coast we liked very much. Unfortunately, the condos we liked we could not afford. Condos on the beach were a quarter of a million dollars and more. The so-called garden condos, away from the beach, started at a hundred and seventy thousand and up. It was not just the cost of buying a condo, it was also the high maintenance fees that were above our budget. So, we gave up.

Then in 1994 I decided that we should try to do a vacation property exchange. We would use our Driggs house as a ski vacation place in exchange for a place somewhere on Florida's seashore. I signed up with a property exchange company and the first booklet I received listed a condo on Hutchinson Island. I called the owner and an exchange was arranged. We had the condo for two weeks in April, and the condo owner spent three weeks in June in Driggs.

Why did we want to go to Hutchinson Island? In 1978 the two Jovanovic families vacationed there. We had stayed in the Holiday Inn, one of the very few buildings on a several-miles-long narrow island. The Island was wild and beautiful. When we got there in 1994 there were still empty stretches of land along the beach, and new condo complexes were still being built. Island Crest condo where we stayed was built in 1982. A nice two-bedroom condo, overlooking the beach was selling for one hundred and twelve thousand dollars. A major difference from anything we had seen before on the Florida's West Coast.

Drasko and I did an analysis of our budget. We decided that we could afford to buy a condo if we rented it during the season, January to March, until we retire. We also had to take into account that Vesna was starting medical school and would need financial help from us.

Luckily she was accepted at University of California Davis Medical School, and as a California resident her tuition was insignificant compared to that of the University of Alabama where she was accepted and was planning to go at the time we did our budgeting.

We met Gloria Roberts, a realtor, who lived in the Island Crest Condominium building. She showed us several condos available in the two buildings in the condo complex. We made an offer on Island Crest condo #509, and left for home. After an unsuccessful negotiation we did not buy it.

I decided to go to Hutchinson Island again in September to look some more. I still had one week coming to me from the property exchange deal. Drasko could not be bothered to go to Florida again, so I asked Marija and Boza Lalevic to join me for a mini vacation. Gloria was expecting me and, after Marija and I had looked at every available condo on the Island, we decided that Island Crest was the best place to be. This time around the owners of condo #509 were more amenable, and by November 1994 we were the proud owners of a fifth floor two-bedroom two-bathroom condo overlooking the Atlantic Ocean.

The condo was rented out during high season until 1998. During the first four years we used the condo off-and-on for short vacations. Since 1998 we have spent the winter months there. Buying the condo was the smartest thing we did for our retirement years.

By now we know many nice people who live in our condo complex. I do pool exercises every day with a group of nice ladies. Our balcony doors in the living room and in our bedroom are wide open all the time. The sound of the ocean waves is music to our ears. The weather is perfect. Most of the time the temperature is in the seventies and eighties with a pleasant ocean breeze. We have two swimming pools, a Jacuzzi and a glorious sandy beach. The best part of being in Florida is that our family and friends like to come and visit. Boza and Marija Lalevic spend a month with us every January. Branka, my sister-in-law, comes for a week in February. Jasna, Tom, Matejas and Lukas come during their spring break. Vesna comes for a week or two. Other friends stop by for a day or two while they vacation somewhere in Florida. And the best part of it all is that the value of the condo has nearly quadrupled since we bought it.

++

After Jasna left for college in 1981, and then Vesna in 1985, we timed our spring vacations to their school breaks. Slowly they stopped coming with us. Drasko and I continued to alternate between Florida beaches and the Caribbean Islands. During the eighties and nineties we went to Longboat Key, Englewood Beach, Don Pedro Island, Hutchinson Island and Venice in Florida; and Tortola, Eleuthera, Tobago, Cayman Islands, Caicos, Antigua and the Dominican Republic.

Vesna recently asked me how I found the places we went to. It was not easy. We always wanted to be on a wild, deserted beach. Early on I had looked at ads in *Yachting* magazine for villas and cottages, thinking that one would have to have a boat to get there. My logic was pretty good. I found most of our Caribbean beach accommodations that way. Later on, I would get the official government information package put out by island countries. I would look at the geography of an island, and would select to go where there were the least numbers of hotels on a beach. That is how I found the villas on Negril in Jamaica, in Providenciales on Caicos, and on Tobago. In Florida I would call a local chamber of commerce and get their booklet of information. Again, I looked for the least populated area to rent a condo. I found Longboat Key, Englewood Beach and Don Pedro Island that way.

It would be hard to find places like that anywhere today. All the beaches we went to are built up by now. For example, when we were on Hutchinson Island in 1978 the Holiday Inn was one of very few buildings on a several-miles-long beach. Today, in 2004, there is very little room left for new construction. Our condo is on a busy road, a mile north of the Holiday Inn. The Island now has hotels, low-rise and high-rise condo buildings, strip malls, two museums and, as of last year, a big Publix supermarket. But when I am in our living room looking out at the ocean I still feel like I am on a wild beach.

++

Thanks to many physics meetings and conferences Drasko saw much more of the world than I did. After he retired he decided he did not want to travel anymore. But, there were places that I still wanted to see. So, I joined my friend Marge Hanson and a group of her friends on several European tours. I went with them to Scandinavia in 1997, to Southwest England in 1999 and on a river cruise from Vienna to Amsterdam in 2001. I would still like to see Spain and Portugal, but there is time.

In 1999, Vesna and I went on a Carnival cruise from Los Angeles to Puerto Vallarta, Mazatlan and Cabo San Lucas. Life on board a two-thousand-or-more passenger ship was great fun, but not something I would do often. The river cruise on a small one-hundred-thirty-passenger ship was much more pleasant for me.

In retrospect, I realize that I have not seen much of the world. I have never been to the Far East, Australia, Africa, or South America. I have never visited Eastern European countries other than Hungary. It was much more important to me to go to Yugoslavia to visit my family as often as I could. Traveling through the United States was always more important to me than beating the streets of some other country. How much did I miss? Probably a lot, but I survived.

++

Visiting Vesna in Portland became a new kind of vacation for Drasko and me. Vesna loved her Pacific Northwest and was eager to show it off. When we were there, every weekend was a mini-vacation. And we were there for quite a long time when I got my new knee there in 2002, and when Drasko got his new hip in 2003. Mt. Hood, Mt. St. Helens, the Oregon Coast, Olympic National Park and more were all within an easy driving distance from Vesna's house.

In spite of everybody's belief the weather in Portland was great all the time while we were there. It may be rainy in January through March, but the rest of the year, when we were there, the weather was sunny and warm. In 2002, when Jasna and her family visited us in

Portland, we spent a part of Thanksgiving week at Cannon Beach on the Oregon Coast. It was sunny and in the seventies. The Pacific Ocean is cold for swimming, but just being on the beach was great fun. We swam in the resort's indoor swimming pool and everybody was happy.

Portland is a vacation place in itself. We cruised on the Willamette River. We went for walks in many wooded parks along the rivers and in the hills. We went to several waterfalls, to the Columbia Gorge fisheries, to the Bonneville Dam and its salmon run and many more places. Visiting the Lundys at their house on the edge of a cliff above the Columbia River Gorge, with the view of Mt. Hood, was a treat in itself.

++

So here I am in deep retirement enjoying life to the fullest. Both Drasko and I are healthy. Minor medical problems creep up on us, but we take care of them as fast as we can. So far Medicare and CIGNA, our secondary medical insurance paid by Fermilab, more-or-less takes care of our medical bills. Social Security, a TIAA annuity and income from other tax deferred retirement accounts provide enough income for us to live comfortably.

I have time to listen to jazz. Since I retired I have acquired a nice library of jazz CDs, covering my favorite periods from the nineteen twenties to the nineteen sixties. A few years ago Drasko gave me for my birthday *Jazz For Dummies*, the best book ever. Since then I have accumulated a small library of books on jazz. I became quite knowledgeable and I am selective in what I listen to. When I am in Urbana I go regularly to the Jazz Forum at the UIUC Music School. There I listen to visiting jazz ensembles or soloists, and the music school's own performers. It is a showcase for jazz students open to the public. I go to other jazz performances at the Krannert Center, where artists like Wynton Marsalis, Dee Dee Bridgewater and Cecil Bridgewater recently performed.

I do not watch television much. Reading is much more fun. I also rarely go to the movies. If there is a film I should see Jasna and

Vesna make sure that I do. Drasko and I go to other concerts and opera performances at the Krannert Center when we are in Urbana. When we are in Portland my cultural vistas are much broader thanks to Vesna planning my life. A highlight a couple of years ago was hearing Tony Bennett perform with the Portland Symphony.

As far as hobbies go I think I have only one that qualifies: knitting. Throughout my life I have loved to knit. I did many pullovers and cardigans in complicated patterns for my children, their friends and others. I have not done any recently, but I may do it again in the future.

I often wonder how I could have worked all my life so much and so hard for others. Being in command of my own time is a great feeling. The trouble is that you have to be retired and old to do so. I hope I will stay healthy and enjoy my retirement life for many more years.

Soon after Drasko settled in at the University of Chicago, he wrote to tell me that it would take five years to get a Ph.D. in physics, and that he was going to do it. Therefore, I had to find a way to join him. I promptly went to the American Embassy to ask the consul how to obtain a visa. He asked me what I did, and I told him I was about to graduate with a B.S. in metallurgical engineering. Then he proceeded to tell me that the only way I could get to the United States was also as a student. Drasko was not in a position to support a wife, and the consul would not give me a tourist visa because I would want to stay as long as Drasko was there. Thus, I embarked on a long and complicated process of trying to figure out where and how to become a student for the sake of a visa.

I wrote to Vera Laska, the foreign student admissions officer at the University of Chicago, and Drasko's friend. Vera explained to me that without a car, there was no way I could physically live with Drasko and attend any other university in the Chicago area but the University of Chicago. She mailed me the application forms for the University of Chicago Graduate School. This must have happened in the fall of 1955. In April 1956, I was accepted with a tuition waiver and a student technician job to support myself. Thus, I became a graduate student without ever planning to be one.

++

I met with my student advisor, Professor Norman H. Nachtrieb, in early June 1956. He recommended that I audit a couple of courses during the summer quarter to improve my understanding of spoken English. I audited two courses; one was taught by an American professor, and the other by a German professor. The German professor I understood perfectly. I found out later that he had a very heavy accent. I had a very hard time understanding the American professor. His words flowed together and I could not hear them separately.

But, by the time the fall quarter started I was pretty okay understanding everybody.

I started attending classes in the fall of 1956. I took two classes each quarter. Some of them were easy, and some of them were so advanced that I could barely follow. But I persevered. I must have been very smart to surmount the challenge of the rigor of the program I was in. My undergraduate education was solid but not up-to-date on the current understanding of the basic structure of matter. I knew very little of atomic structure beyond the existence of electrons and the nucleus. To keep up with my course work I continually had to go back and learn the material that my fellow students already knew. I doubt that my professors were aware of my spotty background, and I obviously managed to do a respectable job with my course work.

The labs were a totally different story. I had far more lab experience than my fellow students. My college education had included five-and-a-half years of afternoon lab work. By the time I arrived at the University of Chicago I had probably done every analysis or experiment found in the standard chemistry and metallurgy textbooks. Actually, throughout my career as a research scientist I loved the lab work the best.

Two years later, in 1958, I received a Master of Science in Physical Chemistry with all the pomp and circumstance the University of Chicago had to offer. I continued as a graduate student waiting for Drasko to finish his Ph. D. Drasko graduated in 1959 and the university offered him a postdoctoral position. The university had to apply for a permanent residency status for Drasko to be able to employ him. The application for Drasko automatically included an application for his wife. After the applications were submitted I did not have to worry anymore about my own student visa. I could stop being a student, and I did.

++

My first job as a student technician was in the analytical chemistry laboratory at the Institute for the Study of Metals. The two years of systematic qualitative and quantitative analyses I had in college back home came in very handy. I was able to do a variety of analyses without any additional training. Myrtle Bachelder was the head of the lab. Most of the time she and I were alone in the lab and I loved it. All the wonderful equipment and every possible reagent were there for my use.

But that did not last long. Somebody in the Institute discovered that I had experience in physical metallurgy, a skill needed in the Institute's metallography laboratory. I was transferred to a lab equipped with the latest in instrumentation I had never seen before, and had only read about. The polishing wheels, high-power microscopes with built-in cameras, a high-power microscope with a built-in instrument for hardness measurements and a fully equipped dark room were all a delight to me. Betty Nielsen, an experienced metallographer, was in charge of the lab. Working with her for the next two years was instructive and pure joy.

Across from the metallography lab was the office of Professor Charles Barrett, whose book *Physical Metallurgy* I had used as a textbook in college back home. To my surprise he was not only alive, but was quite young. For some reason I had assumed that all textbook writers must be very old or dead, and I told him so. He got a good laugh out of that. There were many other famous people in the building. Many of them had been part of the Manhattan Project at Los Alamos that produced the atomic bomb. My student advisor, Professor Norman H. Nachtrieb, and Myrtle Bachelder were both Manhattan Project veterans.

My Master's thesis sponsor was Professor Cyril Stanley Smith. He was a well-known metallurgist, instrumental in building the cone for the atomic bomb dropped on Hiroshima. At that time he was interested in the properties of ternary eutectics and of amorphous nickel films. Under Professor Smith's supervision I did two nice experiments. One became my Master's Thesis entitled *Ternary Eutectics.* The other, "Elastic Modulus of Amorphous Nickel Films," was published in the *Journal of Applied Physics* 32 (1), 121–122 January 1961.

I also did work for Professor Harold C. Urey, the Nobel Prize winner who discovered the element deuterium. He did research on meteorites. I prepared many polished sections of meteorites for his studies. I also did hardness measurements across various mineral grains in meteorite polished sections.

I also spent some time working with Dr. George W. Reed while he was trying to learn some of our laboratory techniques. I later worked with George for twenty-eight years doing research on meteorites and lunar samples at Argonne National Laboratory.

++

In the fall of 1960 we moved to La Jolla, California. Drasko had a new job in the Physics Department at the brand-new University of California San Diego campus, located on the site of the Scripps Institute of Oceanography. Once settled, I walked into Dr. Urey's lab and he promptly hired me as a graduate research assistant. Dr. Urey and a number of other senior scientists we knew at the University of Chicago moved to La Jolla a short time before we did. They were to help establish science departments at the new UCSD. Dr. Urey assigned me to Dr. Gordon Goles, my fellow student from the University of Chicago. Gordon must have arrived just before I did. There was no chemistry laboratory set up for him. He was going to do research on meteorites, and also needed a metallography lab. It was decided that I should fly back to the University of Chicago and scout out George Reed's chemistry lab, the best one in the Nuclear Institute, and Betty Nielson's metallography lab. Then I would design our own labs. I did, and pretty soon we had our own chemistry and metallography labs operating.

Our chemistry lab was in the old building above the beach. Our office space and the metallography lab were in the new blue mosaic science building on the hillside. I was developing chemical procedures for future experiments and preparing polished sections for mineral grain studies. I do not believe we did actual experiments since nothing was published that I am aware of. When I left in 1962 I remember leaving behind a thick notebook full of chemical procedures.

++

After we moved back to Chicago in 1962, and until 1965, I was totally content not working. Jasna was born in June 1963 and I loved being a mother. I had no intention of looking for work. It was actually the first time in my life that I was homebound and I loved it. All my life I had been a student or I worked in a lab. Being a mother, and being at home, opened new vistas for me of continuous joy and the command of my own time. I must have been the only woman among my friends that did not get excited about Betty Friedan's 1963 book, *The Feminine Mystique.* I did not believe I needed to be "liberated."

Then in the spring of 1965 an important event happened that changed the course of my professional life. George Reed, who was a research scientist at the University of Chicago, invited me to come and work with him in his laboratory at the Argonne National Laboratory. He insisted I would be of great help to him even if I worked only twice a week for half a day. When I went to visit his lab, he immediately had me help with an experiment he and Ralph Allen, a graduate student from the University of Wisconsin, were engaged in. I, of course, loved it. Just that short venture into a chemical experiment started me thinking: maybe I could work with George on a less than part time basis. I would keep my lab skills and my professional life active. This way it would be much easier for me to go back to work full-time if I ever wanted to do so.

George's offer to let me work only eight hours a week was very appealing. Being paid was an additional incentive. I could afford to hire a babysitter, and have some time for my work and myself. So, in September 1965, I began working with George at Argonne National Laboratory.

Vesna was born in June 1967. After three weeks at home with the baby I went back to work. George was very aware that I had two little children at home. He made no demands on my time beyond what I was willing to give. Two half days a week were sufficient for me to do a lot of lab work. During the summers, when I was mostly gone, our colleague Ralph Allen was at Argonne working with George. By then Ralph was on the faculty at the University of Virginia. A few years later two half days per week turned into two full days per week. Then in 1979, when Vesna started Junior High School, I increased my work time to three days a week. I worked like that until I retired in 1989. The truth was that George and I did chemistry in the lab and then I did lots of calculations and other paper work at home. By the time my children were in school, I had most of the days to myself and could do a lot of work at home. I produced concentration tables of elements we measured, and various graphic interpretations of the data. George then interpreted the data, and drafted the reports. More often than not, a publication was born that way.

++

In 1965 George submitted a proposal to NASA to analyze lunar samples that the Apollo flights to the moon would bring back. It was five years before we actually received the first lunar samples. In the meantime George continued to do experiments on meteorites similar to those Gordon Goles and I had been developing in La Jolla. Thus, it was easy for me to slip right into George's experiments.

It was George's research interest that determined what kind of experiments we did. I spent most of my time in the lab doing radiochemical analysis on whichever samples George was interested in at the time. While waiting for lunar samples, George and I continued to do experiments on meteorites and metamorphic rocks. We were interested in the thermal history of these extraterrestrial and terrestrial rocks. By measuring mercury concentrations released at different temperatures, in stepwise heating experiments, we were able to infer the thermal processes that these rocks had gone through. Between 1967 and 1969 we published five papers on mercury and one on halogens. The publications were in the *Journal of Geophysical Research*, the *Geochemica and Cosmochemica Acta*, the *Earth and Planetary Science Letters* and the *Journal of Inorganic and Nuclear Chemistry*.

++

In the fall of 1969, at a well-publicized event at the Johnson Space Center in Houston, Texas, George Reed was the second United States scientist to receive Apollo 11 samples for analysis. George and

I were primed and ready to start the experiments. What followed were ten years of intense studies of lunar samples that the Apollo flights brought back. We did similar experiments on numerous lunar basalts, breccias, soils and core samples. Our purpose was to develop a global picture of the volatile and several other elements' concentrations on the moon. Our experimental results allowed us also to infer a possible thermal history of the moon.

The biggest job in getting ready to work with lunar samples was setting up a Nitrogen dry-box in our lab where the lunar samples would be opened and prepared for irradiation. The setup was similar to the boxes used in handling radioactive materials. It took lots of practice before George developed the sensitivity needed to prepare 30 to 100 milligrams of rock or soil samples. It was a tedious procedure requiring the use of heavy rubber gloves. The lunar samples were packaged in nitrogen gas in heavy gauge aluminum cylinders, a few inches long and an inch in diameter. It was tough just to unscrew the cover to remove the lunar sample contained in a capped vial. George would first weigh the whole sample, and then take a chip or a scoop to crush in a mortar. Then he would carefully transfer the crushed sample with a narrow spatula into a specially designed and weighed silica ampoule. The ampoule containing the sample was then weighed again. Melting down a specially designed constriction at the neck of the silica ampoule sealed the sample for irradiation.

It took both of us a day or two to prepare a batch of samples. While George was elbow deep in the rubber gloves, I took notes of the procedure and the measurements he did. The lunar samples were never exposed to terrestrial atmosphere while they were in our possession. Six samples were prepared for an experiment and shipped to Brookhaven National Laboratory to be irradiated at their High Flux Reactor. Once irradiated, the samples were opened to the air and radiochemical analyses were performed. When we measured the isotopes with short half-lives we did the experiments at Brookhaven National Laboratory. The experiments with longer-lived isotopes we did in our own lab at Argonne.

Dr. Jarome Hudis in the Chemistry Department at Brookhaven National Laboratory was our host. He gave us one of his labs to use for the duration of our experiments. Thus, we had our own fully equipped radiochemical lab that we used several times per year for several years. Dr. Hudis, who may have been the Director of the Chemistry Department at that time, also provided us with the services of the Department's counting facilities. That was of great help to us because the short-lived isotopes we measured needed to be recounted in short time intervals. If one of us had had to do the counting, our chemical procedures would have been interrupted, and the whole experiment slowed down.

In our experiments we measured the concentrations of halogens, mercury, osmium, ruthenium and several other elements. The concentrations were in parts-per-million to parts-per-billion. We did six to eight irradiations per year. On average we measured five to ten elements per sample. So, six samples per irradiation would produce thirty to sixty precipitates to be counted as often as needed to provide good decay curves for calculating the concentrations. Counting samples was a very time consuming process. George did most of the counting when we did the experiments at Argonne.

We eventually analyzed over three hundred different lunar samples, including several soil samples from the Russian Luna 16 and Luna 20 unmanned flights.

++

Annual Lunar and Planetary Science Conferences were held at the Johnson Space Center. These conferences were the main forums where the scientific community reported the results of a great variety of lunar samples' studies. Eventually, there were thirteen voluminous, hardcover proceedings that encompassed all the work done on the Apollo samples. In addition to the Proceedings, we reported our results in *Geochemica and Cosmochemica Acta, Science, Science Letters* and *The Moon.*

If I had not been involved with George in lunar studies, I would never have had the opportunity to meet and hear the leading scientists in the multiple fields involved in the Apollo program. I also met many of the Apollo astronauts who joined the conference participants at various official and social gatherings. I even managed to sell Jasna's Campfire Girls cookies to several of the astronauts. I still have two of the astronauts' dollar bills (in those days a box of cookies cost one dollar) with several other astronauts' signatures. They are stored in our safe deposit box.

I thoroughly enjoyed rubbing shoulders with all these great people. Not to mention that I was one of a very few women present at these several-hundred-participants meetings. Actually, our group that consisted of George, an African-American, Ralph Allen, of Norwegian descent, and I, a female, was the most perfectly integrated group of scientists.

The conferences were several days long. We had many opportunities to visit the Space Center facilities, including the lunar samples preparation and storage laboratories. These were ultra-clean labs. To enter, we had to be fully dressed in protective coveralls and head covers. Before we could enter the labs we had to go through a chamber with a clean air shower. A few years later, George was involved in designing the permanent lunar sample facility. I believe that more than eighty percent of the eight hundred thirty-nine pounds of lunar samples returned from the moon were stored there for the future generation of scientists' use.

I still have a box that contains a variety of mementos I brought back from the conferences and the Space Center. I am keeping it all, hoping that someday my grandchildren will like to have them.

++

George was sixty-nine in 1989 when he decided to retire. That gave me a good reason to retire, too. I was ready to dedicate my time to the construction of the Fermilab education center, and to leave my life as a research scientist behind. I was fifty-eight years old when I retired in May 1989. By October 1989 I had a new job as the Manager of Fermilab's Education Office.

But before I could leave Argonne we had to return the lunar samples we had in our possession back to NASA. It took me three months to process the samples and organize their return. Each sample had to have a required history form filled in great detail. We had to account for the amounts we used from each sample for various experiments, and of the disposal of the residual solutions from our experimental procedures. The three hundred-plus lunar samples we had in our possession for nearly twenty years were still in their pristine state. They were never exposed to the terrestrial atmosphere, and thus still in the prime condition for other researchers to use.

Then I had to organize my files. I also compiled four three-ring binders with our reprints and other publications for George, Jasna, Vesna and me to have. After I left I never asked what happened to the volumes of notebooks and files I left behind. By now everything is probably thrown away. But that does not bother me. The results of our research were published and that was all that mattered.

++

Looking back over the twenty-eight years of research, and well over a hundred publications, George and I have the right to be proud of our accomplishments. Our trace element studies on meteorites, lunar samples and terrestrial rocks gave us clues to the origins and processes that shaped our solar system and the earth. The Apollo program years provided plenty of funds for the experiments we wanted to do, and more. Later, when NASA and then NSF funds dried up, we joined the effort Professor Thomas Gold initiated in Sweden to find whether there were sources of primeval methane buried deep in the Scandinavian Shield that could be a potential energy resource.

In retrospect I was comfortable with my responsibilities both at home and at work. I never felt that one took something away from the other. Working with George was a pleasure. I had the best of both worlds: my family and my work.

MY FAMILY: DRASKO, JASNA AND VESNA

I will leave it to Drasko, my husband, and Jasna and Vesna, my daughters, to write their own autobiographies. Here I just want to give a synopsis of their lives, for you to learn how they got to where they are today. I was, of course, heavily involved in their lives, and I am very happy to say that I highly approve of their achievements both in their personal and professional lives. Jasna brought Thomas J. Mackin, her husband, into our family. Then they brought into the world our two wonderful grandsons, Matejas Walter Jovanovic Mackin, on May 6, 1998, and Lukas Milos Jovanovic Mackin, on June 12, 2000.

⧢

Drasko was born on May 24, 1930 in Belgrade, Yugoslavia. He grew up in Belgrade at Kralja Petra 91 (King Peter Street 91). After WWII, the street name was changed to 7 July, a public holiday of the Federal Peoples' Republic of Yugoslavia. In 1949 he graduated from the First Boys' High School in Belgrade. In 1953 he received a B. S. degree in physics from the University of Belgrade. During his student years, and after he graduated, he worked at the Nuclear Institute at Vinca. Drasko served in the Yugoslav army from September 1953 until June 1954. While he was in the army, Vinca selected Drasko to receive a stipend provided by the American Technical Assistance for the Undeveloped Nations to study in the United States. These fellowships were offered to students in the Third World developing countries. To be able to leave on time for America, Drasko was released early from the army. We got married four weeks before he left.

On September 11, 1954, Drasko was on the way to the University of Chicago where, he thought, he was going to spend a year specializing in physics. He took a train from Belgrade to Paris, France, and then flew on Air France from Paris to New York. The Yugoslav Atomic Energy Commission paid for his trip. He spent a day in Washington, DC, where he found out that the stipends by the American Technical Assistance did not exist anymore. Financially he was on his own with whatever little money he had brought with him from Yugoslavia. When he arrived at the University of Chicago, he found out he was going to be a graduate student. The University awarded Drasko a tuition waiver and gave him a student technician job. His salary was enough for him to live humbly, but comfortably.

The University of Chicago Physics Department faculty had many Nobel Prize winners and Manhattan Project veterans. Enrico Fermi, Herbert Anderson, Samuel Allison, Gregor Wentzel, Subrahmanyan Chandrasekhar, Maria Goeppert Meyer and others became Drasko's professors. As far as Drasko was concerned, he was in physics heaven and had no intentions of going back home to Yugoslavia until he had graduated with a Ph. D. degree. I joined him in 1956, also as a University of Chicago graduate student.

Drasko received his Ph. D. in 1959 and stayed for an additional year at the University as a post-doc. In 1960 we moved to La Jolla, California. There he was an Assistant Research Physicist at the University of California San Diego. In 1962 he accepted an Associate Physicist position at Argonne National Laboratory in Argonne, Illinois. There he was involved in the construction and commissioning of the Zero Gradient Synchrotron. For the next ten years Drasko did experiments in particle physics using the ZGS.

In 1972 Drasko joined the National Accelerator Laboratory in Batavia, Illinois. He thinks of himself as one of the founders of what later became known as Fermilab-Fermi National Accelerator Laboratory. In 1997 he retired as a Physicist III, the highest rank achieved at Fermilab. Today, he has an Emeritus position and still has an office there. During his tenure at Fermilab he held several positions. He was the Head of C-Zero, the Head of the Physics Division, then for a while he was in the Laboratory Director's Office. He participated in numerous committees, workshops and summer schools. These took him all over the United States and beyond. Many of these trips became great vacations for our family.

Throughout his life Drasko's passion has been teaching physics to young people. At Fermilab he was instrumental in creating Saturday Morning Physics for High School Students. Later, he took part in developing and teaching many physics programs offered by Fermilab's Education Office. For many years he taught physics for non-science majors at Northwestern University, the University of Chicago and the University of Illinois at Champaign-Urbana.

Drasko plays self-taught piano with zest. For a while he also painted and did woodcarving. Since he retired, Drasko reads and thinks about physics. He worries about the United States' foreign policy, especially as they pertain to the former Yugoslavia and current Serbia and Montenegro. Today, at the age of seventy-three, his three major loves are his children and grandchildren, being in Driggs close to the Grand Tetons and being on our beach in Florida.

++

Jasna Diane Jovanovic was born on June 5, 1963 in Chicago, Illinois. She grew up in Downers Grove, Illinois, where we had moved in 1966. She graduated from Downers Grove North High School in 1981. Then in 1985 Jasna received a B. S. in Psychology from the University of Illinois Urbana-Champaign. She continued her education at Pennsylvania State University in State College, Pennsylvania, where in 1991 she received a Ph. D. degree in Human Development and Family Studies. In 1987 Jasna received a Fulbright-Hays Fellowship and a fellowship from the International Research and Exchange Board that made it possible for her to spend a year doing a part of her dissertation research in Belgrade, Yugoslavia. There she made a comparative study on the factors influencing children's math and science achievement.

Another fellowship from the American Association of University Women made it possible for Jasna to write her dissertation in Santa Barbara, California, where, in 1990, she joined her then boyfriend, Tom Mackin. Tom was already a post-doc there.

Jasna and Tom were married on June 19, 1992, in a three-day celebration at Gintaras, a resort on Lake Michigan in Union Pier,

Michigan. Since 1993 both Jasna and Tom have been on the faculty at the University of Illinois Urbana-Champaign. Today, in 2004, Jasna and Tom are Associate Professors at UIUC. Jasna is in the Department of Human and Community Development. Tom is in the Department of Mechanical and Industrial Engineering.

Jasna, Tom, Matejas (I call him Matko, they call him Tej) and Lukas (I call him Lule, they call him Luki) live in Yankee Ridge, a beautiful subdivision in Urbana. They have a modern architect-designed home with a big yard and a swimming pool. A prairie park and a small forest surround their house. Within the forest there is a small lake great for swimming and fishing. With Mary Arriola, who looks after Matko and Lule, they all lead a full, productive and happy life. Matko attends kindergarten at Countryside School, a private school in Champaign, Illinois. Lule is in preschool at the University of Illinois Child Development Lab.

The best part is that our house, also in Yankee Ridge, is two blocks away.

++

Vesna Ann Jovanovic was born on June 21, 1967 in Hinsdale, Illinois. Vesna had an unusual career path. In her early teens Vesna developed a love for movies. She watched old movies on television and read a variety of books on film. After her junior year in high school Vesna decided that she wanted to study film. I felt that she needed to find out what studying film really meant, so I helped her find a summer course in film and television production at the University of California Los Angeles. She loved the course, and when the time came she applied to three film schools and was accepted at New York University Tisch School of Arts in New York.

While at NYU she spent every summer working in the film industry in Hollywood, California. Vesna graduated in seven semesters and in February 1989 she moved to Los Angeles and a job at Paramount Pictures. In May 1989 our whole family was in New York for Vesna's graduation at NYU where she received a B. F. A. degree.

I visited Vesna many times both in New York and then in Santa Monica, where she lived in a high-rise building right on the beach. It was a very pleasant and nice way to live. A year or so into her film career Vesna started questioning the quality of her life working in the film industry. The industry proved to be too much of a commercial and much less of a creative enterprise, and the hours were horrendous.

Vesna's disillusionment peaked in the summer of 1990, and she decided to look for another career. In September 1990, while she was visiting Jasna and Tom in Santa Barbara, she applied for several jobs there. She got a job at *Islands* magazine and moved to Santa Barbara. She was happy living without the film industry stress, and besides, Jasna and Tom lived nearby.

Six month into the job at *Islands* Vesna started searching again. After a year she decided to pursue a career in medicine. She quit her job and enrolled at Santa Barbara Community College. It took her two years to take all the science and math courses she needed to be able to apply to a medical school.

In the fall of 1994 Vesna became a medical student at the University of California Davis.

After she graduated in 1998, she did a three-year residency program in family practice at the Southwest Medical Center in Vancouver, Washington. She finished in June 2001 and after a great summer traveling abroad Vesna started her medical practice. She is now, in 2004, in her third year as a family physician in Portland, Oregon.

EPILOGUE

Today is March 21, 2004, and I am in Florida. I am about to finish writing this book. It is six-thirty in the morning. I should be done by nine-thirty. Then from ten to a quarter of eleven I will join other ladies in the swimming pool for our daily exercises. Then I will sit in the sun and read till noon. Then I will come back up, have lunch, check my mail and email and then work for a while on the revisions of the Island Crest Condominium Bylaws.

The Condo Association was struggling to operate under the outdated bylaws written in 1979. Two other condo owners and I volunteered to be on the bylaws review committee. So far we have met twice for two hours, and we are already half done. I am the committee chair, so it is up to me to keep a running update of our proposed revisions, and that takes time. I have done similar work before for the Horseshoe Creek Association, the Teewinot Homeowners Association, the Ponds of Windsor Homeowners Association and Friends of Fermilab. I felt that I should help this group too.

I will go back down to the pool or to the beach around three in the afternoon. I will sit in the sun and read some more, and then I will do my ten-lap swim. There will be people there I know, so I will chat a little, too. I will come back up to our fifth floor condo around four-thirty, and I will get on the computer, while Drasko cooks dinner. We will eat around five-thirty and watch the *BBC World News* and *The News Hour*. Later I will clean the kitchen, read and be in bed by nine-thirty or ten.

Jasna, Tom, Matko and Lule will arrive later today and stay for a week. Then Vesna will arrive next Thursday, and our whole family will be together for four days. Vesna will stay with us until next Friday. After she leaves, I will slowly begin to get the condo ready for our departure. All minor repairs will be done, the carpets will be washed, the refrigerator will be emptied, our stuff that we leave here will be packed and stored, our mail forwarded, our subscriptions' mailing address changed again and more. It goes like this every time we leave any one of our homes in Florida, Illinois, or Idaho.

Well, I will say goodbye. It is going to be a gorgeous sunny, eighty-degree day again.

A NOTE ON NAMES AND PRONOUNCIATIONS

Definitions

<u>Serbian — English</u>

Cika (Čika) — Uncle, also a general address of respect of close family friends

Tetka–Teta — Aunt, also a general address of respect of close family friends

Serbian Spelling and Pronunciation

(ž = zh (Zhivago); č = hard ch; ć = soft ch; š = sh)

<u>People</u>

Boza — Boža

Bozidar — Božidar

Bosko — Boško

Carnic — Čarnić

Ceda — Čeda

Cedomilj — Čedomilj

Cedomir — Čedomir

Cika — Čika

Dimitrijevic — Dimitrijević

(same for all last names ending in "ic")

Drasko — Draško

Kaca — Kaća

Milos — Miloš

Misa — Miša

Miska — Miška

Sasa — Saša

Sipos — Šipoš

Skolnik — Školnik

Tosa — Toša

Vucic — Vučić

Zarko — Žarko

<u>Places</u>

Basko Polje — Baško Polje

Milocer — Miločer

Pancevo — Pančevo

Porec — Poreč

Soca — Soča

Vinca — Vinča

Vrsic — Vršic

Patrijarsija — Patrijaršija

JOVANOVIC FAMILY TREE
2008

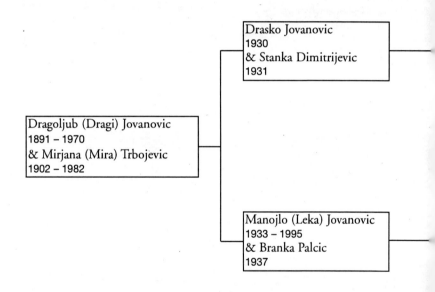

Drasko Jovanovic
1930
& Stanka Dimitrijevic
1931

Dragoljub (Dragi) Jovanovic
1891 – 1970
& Mirjana (Mira) Trbojevic
1902 – 1982

Manojlo (Leka) Jovanovic
1933 – 1995
& Branka Palcic
1937

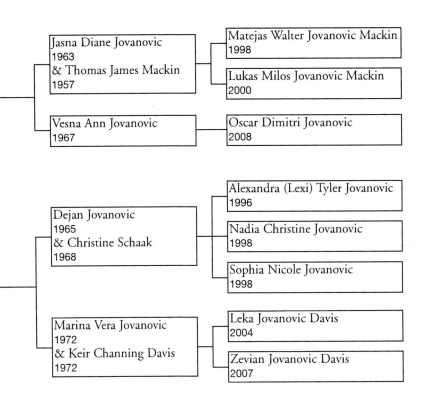

Jasna Diane Jovanovic
1963
& Thomas James Mackin
1957

Matejas Walter Jovanovic Mackin
1998

Lukas Milos Jovanovic Mackin
2000

Vesna Ann Jovanovic
1967

Oscar Dimitri Jovanovic
2008

Dejan Jovanovic
1965
& Christine Schaak
1968

Alexandra (Lexi) Tyler Jovanovic
1996

Nadia Christine Jovanovic
1998

Sophia Nicole Jovanovic
1998

Marina Vera Jovanovic
1972
& Keir Channing Davis
1972

Leka Jovanovic Davis
2004

Zevian Jovanovic Davis
2007

ARGONNE NATIONAL LABORATORY:
A LETTER OF RECOMMENDATION

JUSTIFICATION FOR EMPLOYMENT
AT ARGONNE NATIONAL LABORATORY

FROM: Argonne National Laboratory   DATE: November 5, 1982
9700 South Cass Avenue
Argonne, Illinois 60479
312/972-3585

TO: Ellis P. Steinberg
Director, Chemistry Division

SUBJECT: Employment of Stanka Jovanovic by ANL

I wish to elaborate on justification for employment of Stanka Jovanovic and on the items on need for service, skills and experience, etc., requested in the Policy Manual.

Stanka Jovanovic is expert in various areas of geochemistry as the result of 18 years of research in this field at ANL as well as earlier work at the Metals Institute at The University of Chicago and in Professor Urey's group at the University of California at San Diego. The high productivity of our group is to a significant degree the result of this expertise. My productivity will be reduced if the support and contribution of S. Jovanovic are not available.

S. Jovanovic has extensive familiarity with the pertinent literature and with the materials selected for investigation. She is highly competent in correlating new data obtained in our laboratory with those existing in the literature and in proposing new approaches and solutions to problems being studied. She provides the total familiarity and close coordination required by the highly structured and time dependent nature of the laboratory procedures used. Her skills in activation analysis techniques, utilization of other sources of analytical data, experience in ultra clean sample handling procedures are essential for our research.

I certify that the services of Mrs. Jovanovic are essential for the pursuit of the research conducted by our group. It is important to note that S. Jovanovic is co-author of three present proposals as well as many in the past and usually has been the sole collaborator on research reported in over 80 publications.

There is no one else in the Laboratory with the necessary background breadth of experience, familiarity with the field or familiarity with the sample inventory (several hundred lunar, meteoritic and terrestrial samples), the database and the detailed records utilized by the group. No other group in the Chicago area or elsewhere addresses the specific range of subjects studied by our group (see appended bibliography).

George W. Reed, Jr.

ARGONNE NATIONAL LABORATORY:
A LIST OF SCIENTIFIC PUBLICATIONS
1961–1988

ELASTIC MODULUS OF AMORPHOUS NICKEL FILMS
S. Jovanovic and C. S. Smith
J. Appl. Phys. 32 (1), 121–122 (January 1961)

MERCURY IN CHONDRITES
G. W. Reed, Jr. and S. Jovanovic
J. Geophys. Res. 72 (8), 2219–2228 (April 15,1967)

Hg IN METAMORPHIC ROCKS
S. Jovanovic and G. W. Reed, Jr.
Geochim. Cosmochim. Acta 32, 341–346 (1968)

MERCURY ABUNDANCES AND THERMAL HISTORY OF METEORITES
G. W. Reed, Jr. and S. Jovanovic
Origin and Distribution of the Elements, L. H. Ahrens, Ed., Pergamon Press,
1968, pp. 321–328

SOME HALOGEN MEASUREMENTS OF ACHONDRITES
G. W. Reed, Jr. and S. Jovanovic
Earth Planet. Sci. Lett. 6 (4), 316–320 (July 1969)

Hg ISOTOPIC MEASUREMENTS IN CHONDRITES
G. W. Reed, Jr. and S. Jovanovic
Meteoritics 4 (3), 204–205 (1969)

196Hg AND 202Hg ISOTOPIC RATIOS IN CHONDRITES
G. W. Reed, Jr. and S. Jovanovic
J. Inorg. Nucl. Chem. 31, 3783–3788 (December 1969)

HALOGENS, MERCURY, LITHIUM AND OSMIUM IN
APOLLO 11 SAMPLES
G. W. Reed, Jr. and S. Jovanovic
Proc. Apollo 11 Lunar Sci. Conf.2 Geochim. Cosmochim. Acta, Pergamon
Press, London, 1970, pp. 1487–1492

TRACE ELEMENTS AND ACCESSORY MINERALS IN LUNAR SAMPLES
G. W. Reed, Jr., S. Jovanovic, and L. H. Fuchs
Science 167 (3918), 501–503 (January 30.1970)

HALOGENS, MERCURY, LITHIUM AND URANIUM IN
APOLLO 12 SAMPLES
S. Jovanovic and G. W. Reed,
Jr. Trans. Am. Geophys. Union 51, 585 (July 1970)

THE HALOGENS AND OTHER TRACE ELEMENTS IN APOLLO 12
SAMPLES AND THE IMPLICATIONS OF HALIDES, PLATINUM
METALS, AND MERCURY ON SURFACES
G. W. Reed, Jr. and S. Jovanovic
Proc. 2nd Lunar Sci. Conf.2, MIT Press, Cambridge, Massachusetts, 1971,
pp. 1261–1276

SURFACE-RELATED MERCURY IN LUNAR SAMPLES
G. W. Reed, Jr., J. A. Goleb, and S. Jovanovic
Science 172, 258–261 (April 16, 1971)

FLUORINE AND OTHER TRACE ELEMENTS IN LUNAR
PLAGIOCLASE CONCENTRATES
G. W. Reed, Jr., S. Jovanovic, and L. H. Fuchs
Earth Planet. Sci. Lett. 11, 354–358 (1971)

204Pb IN APOLLO 14 SAMPLES
R. O. Allen, Jr., S. Jovanovic, and G. W. Reed, Jr.
Lunar Science III, Revised Abstracts of Papers, 3rd Lunar Science Conference,
Houston, Texas, January 10–13, 1972, C. Watkins, Ed., Lunar Science
Institute Contribution No. 88, 1972, pp. 15–17

CONCENTRATIONS AND LABILITY OF THE HALOGENS, PLATINUM
METALS AND MERCURY IN APOLLO 14 AND 15 SAMPLES
G. W. Reed, Jr., S. Jovanovic, and L. H. Fuchs
Lunar Science III, Revised Abstracts of Papers, 3rd Lunar Science Conference,
Houston, Texas, January 10–13, 1972, C. Watkins, Ed., Lunar Science
Institute Contribution No. 88, 1972, pp. 637–639

204Pb IN APOLLO 14 SAMPLES AND INFERENCES
REGARDING PRIMORDIAL Pb LUNAR GEOCHEMISTRY
R. O. Allen, Jr., S. Jovanovic, and G. W. Reed, Jr.
Proc. 3rd Lunar Sci. Conf., Geochim. Cosmochim. Acta 2, Supple 3,
1645–1650 (1972)

TRACE ELEMENTS RELATIONS BETWEEN APOLLO 14 AND 15 AND
OTHER LUNAR SAMPLES, AND THE IMPLICATIONS OF A MOON-
WIDE CL-KREEP COHERENCE AND Pt-METAL NONCOHERENCE
G. W. Reed, Jr., S. Jovanovic, and L. H. Fuchs
Proc. 3rd Lunar Sci. Conf., Geochim. Cosmochim. Acta 2, Supple 3,
1989–2001 (1972)

CONCENTRATIONS AND THERMAL RELEASE OF Hg FROM IRON
AND ZINC SULFIDES
G. W. Reed, Jr., S. Jovanovic, and A. C. Tennissen
Earth Planet. Sci. Lett. 14, 26–30 (1972)

FRACTIONATED TRACE ELEMENTS IN LUNAR ROCKS AND SOILS
G. W. Reed, Jr.
Trans. Am. Nucl. Soc. 15 (1), 139 (June 1972)

TRACE ELEMENT COMPARISONS BETWEEN MARE AND
APENNINE-FRONT NONMARE SAMPLES
G. W. Reed, Jr. and S. Jovanovic
The Apollo 15 Lunar Samples, J. W. Chamberlain and C. Watkins, Eds.,
The Lunar Science Institute, Houston, Texas, October 6,1972, pp. 247–249

TRACE ELEMENT PROFILES, NOTABLY Hg, FROM A PRELIMINARY
STUDY OF THE APOLLO 15 DEEP-DRILL CORE
S. Jovanovic and G. W. Reed, Jr.
Earth Planet. Sci. Lett. 16, 257–262 (1972)

COMPARATIVE STUDY OF THE DISTRIBUTION OF TRACE
ELEMENTS IN METEORITIC MATTER
S. Jovanovic and G. W. Reed, Jr.
Meteoritics 8 (1), 47 (1973)

LUNAR FLUORINE AND FLUORAPATITE
G. W. Reed, Jr. and S. Jovanovic
Meteoritics 8 (1), 65 (1973)

PRIMORDIAL Pb IN APOLLO 15 SAMPLES
R. O. Allen, Jr., S. Jovanovic, and G. W. Reed, Jr.
Lunar Science IV, J. W. Chamberlain and C. Watkins, Eds., Lunar Science
Institute, Houston, Texas, 1973, pp. 34–37

TRACE ELEMENT STUDIES ON APOLLO 16 SAMPLES
S. Jovanovic and G. W. Reed, Jr.
Lunar Science IV, J. W. Chamberlain and C. Watkins, Eds., Lunar Science
Institute, Houston, Texas, 1973, pp. 418–420

THE HALOGENS, U, Li, Te AND P2O5 IN FIVE APOLLO 17
SOIL SAMPLES
S. Jovanovic, K. Jensen, and G. W. Reed, Jr.
Trans. Am. Geophys. Union 54 (6), 595 (June 1973)

THE HALOGENS IN LUNA 16 AND LUNA 20 SOILS
G. W. Reed, Jr. and S. Jovanovic
Geochim. Cosmochim. Acta 37 (4), 1007–1009 (1973)

FLUORINE IN LUNAR SAMPLES: IMPLICATIONS CONCERNING
LUNAR FLUORAPATITE
G. W. Reed, Jr. and S. Jovanovic
Geochim. Cosmochim. Act 37, 1457–1462 (1973)

FOURTH LUNAR SCIENCE CONFERENCE
G. W. Reed, Jr. et al. Science 181, 615–622 (August 17, 1973)

LUNAR BULK SAMPLE TRACE ELEMENT CONTENTS AND KREEP
G. W. Reed, Jr. and S. Jovanovic
The Moon 8, 176–181 (1973)

GEOCHEMISTRY OF PRIMORDIAL Pb, Bi AND Zn IN APOLLO
15 SAMPLES
R. O. Allen, Jr., S. Jovanovic, and G. W. Reed, Jr.
Proc. 4th Lunar Sci. Conf., Geochim. Cosmochim. Acta 2, Supple 4,
1169–1176 (1973)

VOLATILE TRACE ELEMENTS AND THE CHARACTERIZATION OF
THE CAYLEY FORMATION AND THE PRIMITIVE LUNAR CRUST
S. Jovanovic and G. W. Reed, Jr.
Proc. 4th Lunar Sci. Conf., Geochim. Cosmochim. Acta 2, Supple 4,
1313–1324 (1973)

PRE- OR POST- ACCRETIONAL DISTRIBUTION OF TRACE ELEMENTS
S. Jovanovic and G. W. Reed, Jr.
Meteoritics 8 (4), (1974)

204Pb, Bi, Tl AND Zn IN APOLLO 16 SAMPLES AND INFERENCES ON
THE LUNAR GEOCHEMISTRY OF 204Pb BASED ON METEORITIC
AND TERRESTRIAL SAMPLE STUDIES
R. O. Allen, Jr., S. Jovanovic, D. Showalter, and G. W. Reed, Jr.
Lunar Science V, Lunar Science Institute, Houston, Texas, 1974, pp. 12–14

LABILE TRACE ELEMENTS IN APOLLO 17 SAMPLES
S. Jovanovic and G. W. Reed, Jr.
Lunar Science V, Lunar Science Institute, Houston, Texas, 1974, pp. 391–393

A STUDY OF 204Pb PARTITION IN LUNAR SAMPLES USING TERRES-
TRIAL AND METEORITIC ANALOGUES
R. O. Allen, Jr., S. Jovanovic, and G. W. Reed, Jr.
Geochim. Cosmochim. Acta 2, Supple 5, 1617–1623 (1974)

LABILE AND NON-LABILE ELEMENT RELATIONSHIPS AMONG
APOLLO 17 SAMPLES
S. Jovanovic and G. W. Reed, Jr.
Geochim. Cosmochim. Acta 2, Supple 5, 1685–1701 (1974)

HALOGENS AND OTHER TRACE ELEMENTS IN STATION 2
BOULDER SAMPLES
S. Jovanovic and G. W. Reed, Jr.
Interdisciplinary Studies of Samples from Boulder 1, Station 2, Apollo 17,
Consortium Indomitabile, Vol. 2, Smithsonian Astrophysical Observatory,
Cambridge, Massachusetts, pp. X-l–X-6, November 12, 1974

BROMINE IN THE LUNAR ATMOSPHERE
S. Jovanovic and G. W. Reed, Jr.
Meteoritics 9 (4), 357–359 (December 30, 1974)

HEAVY ELEMENT AFFINITIES IN APOLLO 17 SAMPLES
R. O. Allen, Jr., S. Jovanovic, and G. W. Reed, Jr.
Earth Planet. Sci. Lett.27, 163–169 (1975)

CL AND P205 SYSTEMATICS: CLUES TO EARLY LUNAR MAGMAS
S. Jovanovic and G. W. Reed, Jr.
Proc. Lunar Sci. Conf. 6th, Geochim. Cosmochim. Acta, Suppl. 6,
1737–1751 (1975)

SOIL BRECCIA RELATIONSHIPS AND VAPOR DEPOSITS ON
THE MOON
S. Jovanovic and G. W. Reed, Jr.
Proc. Lunar Sci. Conf. 6th, Geochim. Cosmochim. Acta, Suppl. 6, pp.
1753–1759 (1975)

AGGLUTINATES: ROLE IN ELEMENT AND ISOTOPE CHEMISTRY
AND INFERENCES REGARDING VOLATILE-RICH ROCK 66095
AND GLASS 74220
R. O. Allen, Jr., S. Jovanovic, and G. W. Reed, Jr.
Proc. Lunar Sci. Conf. 6th, Geochim. Cosmochim. Acta, Suppl. 6, pp.
2271–2279 (1975)

HISTORY OF BOULDER 1 AT STATION 2, APOLLO 17 BASED ON
TRACE ELEMENT INTERRELATIONSHIPS
S. Jovanovic and G. W. Reed, Jr.
The Moon 14, 385–393 (1975)

NEW RESULTS ON ISOTOPICALLY ANOMALOUS Hg
S. Jovanovic and G. W. Reed, Jr.
Trans. Am. Geophys. Union 57 (4), 278 (April 1976) Abstract P59

INTERRELATIONS AMONG ISOTOPICALLY ANOMALOUS MERCURY
FRACTIONS FROM METEORITES AND POSSIBLE COSMOLOGICAL
INFERENCES
S. Jovanovic and G. W. Reed, Jr.
Science 193, 888–891 (3 September 1976)

A CASE FOR A COSMIC COMPLEMENT OF SIDEROPHILE ELEMENTS
IN THE MOON
S. Jovanovic and G. W. Reed, Jr.
Meteoritics 11 (4), 306–307 (1976)

196Hg AND 202Hg ISOTOPIC RATIOS IN CHONDRITES: REVISITED
S. Jovanovic and G. W. Reed, Jr.
Earth Planet. Sci. Lett. 31, 95–100 (1976)

CHEMICAL FRACTIONATION OF Ru AND Os IN THE MOON
S. Jovanovic and G. W. Reed, Jr.
Proc. Lunar Sci. Conf. 7th, Geochim. Cosmochim. Acta, Suppl. 7, pp.
3437–3446 (1976)

CONVECTION CELLS IN THE EARLY LUNAR MAGMA OCEAN:
TRACE-ELEMENT EVIDENCE
S. Jovanovic and G. W. Reed, Jr.
Proc. Lunar Sci. Conf. 7th, Geochim. Cosmochim. Acta, Suppl. 7, pp.
3447–3459 (1976)

Hg AND Os ISOTOPIC VARIATIONS IN LUNAR BRECCIAS
S. Jovanovic and G. W. Reed, Jr.
Trans. Am. Geophys. Union 58 (6), 431 (June 1977) Abstract P52

IS OSMIUM CHEMICALLY FRACTIONATED IN THE MOON?
A RESPONSE
S. Jovanovic and G. W. Reed, Jr.
Proc. Lunar Sci. Conf. 8th, pp. 53–56 (1977)

TRACE ELEMENT GEOCHEMISTRY AND THE EARLY LUNAR
DIFFERENTIATION
S. Jovanovic and G. W. Reed, Jr.
Proc. Lunar Sci. Conf. 8th, pp. 623–632 (1977)

VOLATILE METAL DEPOSITS ON LUNAR SOIL—
RELATION TO VOLCANISM
G. W. Reed, Jr., R. O. Allen, Jr., and S. Jovanovic
Proc. Lunar Sci. Conf. 8th, pp. 3917–3930 (1977)

METEORITE CARBON RESIDUES: VOLATILIZED-Hg AND
OTHER ELEMENTS
8. Jovanovic and G. W. Reed, Jr.
Trans. Am. Geophys. Union 59 (4), 314 (April 1978) Abstract P33

Hg AND SIDEROPHILE ELEMENTS IN METEORITE CARBON
RESIDUES
S. Jovanovic and G. W. Reed, Jr.
Meteoritics 13, 508–511 (1978)

LUNA 24 ORIGINS: SOME TRACE ELEMENT CONSTRAINTS
S. Jovanovic, K. J. Jensen, and G. W. Reed, Jr.
Mare Crisium: The View from Luna 24, R. B. Merrill and J. J. Papike, Eds.,
Pergamon Press, New York, 1978, pp. 695–700

TRACE ELEMENT EVIDENCE FOR A LATERALLY INHOMOGENEOUS
MOON
S. Jovanovic and G. W. Reed, Jr. Proc.
Lunar Planet. Sci. Conf. 9th, pp. 59–80 (1978)

PRIMORDIAL Pb, RADIOGENIC Pb AND LUNAR SOIL MATURATION
G. W. Reed, Jr. and S. Jovanovic
Proc. Lunar Planet. Sci. Conf. 9th, pp. 2215–2220 (1978)

Cl AND P205 IN MINERAL SEPARATES FROM A LUNAR BASALT
S. Jovanovic and G. W. Reed, Jr.
Lunar and Planetary Science X, Part 2, 633–635 (1979)

LUNAR REGOLITH EVOLUTION: A LOW-TEMPERATURE VOLATILE
ELEMENT PERSPECTIVE
S. Jovanovic and G. W. Reed, Jr.
Lunar and Planetary Science X, Part 2, 636–638 (1979)

TRACE ELEMENTS IN ALLENDE CARBON-RESIDUE
RELATED PHASES—A CONTAMINATION CONTROL
EXPERIMENT
S. Jovanovic and G. W. Reed, Jr.
Lunar and Planetary Science X, Part 2, 639–640 (1979)

VOLATILE AND REFRACTORY METALS IN METEORITE CARBON-
RICH RESIDUES
S. Jovanovic and G. W. Reed, Jr.
Meteoritics 14 (4), 437 (1979)

REGOLITH LAYERING PROCESSES BASED ON STUDIES OF LOW-
TEMPERATURE VOLATILE ELEMENTS IN APOLLO CORE SAMPLES
S. Jovanovic and G. W. Reed, Jr.
Proc. Lunar Planet. Sci. Conf. 10th, pp. 1425–1435 (1979)

NEAR-SURFACE DAYTIME THERMAL CONDUCTIVITY IN THE
LUNAR REGOLITH
G. W. Reed, Jr. and S. Jovanovic
Proc. Lunar Planet. Sci. Conf. 10th, pp. 1637–1647 (1979)

RARE EARTH ELEMENTS IN ACID LEACHES AND RESIDUES
FROM WHOLE ROCK AND MINERAL SEPARATES FROM LUNAR
BASALT 75055
S. Jovanovic and G. W. Reed, Jr.
Meteoritics 15 (4), 310 (1980)

CANDIDATE SAMPLES FOR THE EARLIEST LUNAR CRUST
S. Jovanovic and G. W. Reed, Jr.
Proc. Conf. Lunar Highlands Crust, Geochim. Cosmochim. Acta, Supple.
12, 1980, pp. 101–111

Hg AND PT-METALS IN METEORITE CARBON-RICH RESIDUES:
SUGGESTIONS FOR POSSIBLE HOST PHASE FOR Hg
S. Jovanovic and G. W. Reed, Jr.
Geochim. Cosmochim. Act 44, 1399–1407 (1980)

Cl, P205, U AND Br ASSOCIATED WITH MINERAL
SEPARATES FROM A LOW AND A HIGH Ti MARE BASALT
S. Jovanovic and G. W. Reed, Jr.
Proc. Lunar Planet. Sci. Conf. 11th, pp. 125–134 (1980)

ELEMENT MOBILITIES RELATED TO ALTERATION OF GRANITE
FROM A IDHP CORE
S. Jovanovic and G. W. Reed, Jr.
EOS 62 (17), 389 (April 28, 1981)

NOBLE METAL SITES IN ALLENDE—CHEMICAL EVIDENCE
S. Jovanovic and G. W. Reed, Jr.
Meteoritics 16 (4), 334–335 (1981)

ASPECTS OF THE HISTORY OF 66095 BASED ON TRACE ELEMENTS
IN CLASTS AND WHOLE ROCK
S. Jovanovic and G. W. Reed, Jr.
Proc. Lunar Planet. Sci. Conf. 12B, pp. 295–304 (1981)

THE SIGNIFICANCE OF Cl/P205 RATIOS FROM LUNAR
SAMPLES—A RESPONSE
G. W. Reed, Jr. and S. Jovanovic
Proc. Lunar Planet. Sci. Conf. 12B, pp. 333–336 (1981)

THE ROLE OF PHOSPHORUS IN LUNAR SAMPLES—
A CHEMICAL STUDY
S. Jovanovic and G. W. Reed, Jr.
EOS 63, 1350 (December 28, 1982)

THE ROLE OF PHOSPHORUS IN LUNAR SAMPLES—
A CHEMICAL STUDY
S. Jovanovic and G. W. Reed, Jr.
Proc. 13th Lunar Planet. Sci. Conf., J. Geophys. Res. 88, Supplement,
Part 2, A705–A712 (February 15,1983)

TRAPPING OF GASES AND LOW TEMPERATURE VOLATILES IN
LUNAR SAMPLES
S. Jovanovic and G. W. Reed, Jr.
Conference on Planetary Volatiles, Alexandria, Minnesota, October 9–12,
1982, LPT Tech. Report 83–01, pp. 94–98

METEORITE Hg DIFFUSION STUDIES
S. Jovanovic and G. W. Reed, Jr.
Meteoritic 19 (4), 248–250 (1984)

METEORITE Hg DIFFUSION STUDIES II—INFERENCES REGARDING
METEORITE THERMAL EVENTS
S. Jovanovic and G. W. Reed, Jr.
Meteoritics 20 (4), 675–676 (1985)

THE THERMAL RELEASE OF Hg FROM CHONDRITES AND THEIR
THERMAL HISTORIES
S. Jovanovic and G. W. Reed, Jr.
Geochim. Cosmochim. Act 49, 1743–1751 (1985)

Hg GEOTHERMOMETRY: FURTHER APPLICATIONS
S. Jovanovic and G. W. Reed, Jr.
Meteoritics 21 (4), 409 (1986)

Hg CONCENTRATIONS IN AND GEOTHERMOMETRY OF
ANTARCTIC ACHONDRITES
S. Jovanovic and G. W. Reed, Jr.
Meteoritics 22 (4), 423–424 (1987)

ISOTOPICALLY ANOMALOUS Hg IN ANTARCTIC METEORITES
S. Jovanovic and G. W. Reed, Jr.
Meteoritics 22 (4), 424–425 (1987)

ISOTOPICALLY ANOMALOUS 196Hg AND 202Hg IN ANTARCTIC
ACHONDRITES
S. Jovanovic and G. W. Reed, Jr.
Geophys. Res. Lett. 14 (11), 1127–1130 (November 1987

TRACE ELEMENTS IN GRAVBERG DRILLHOLE SAMPLES
S. Jovanovic and G. W. Reed, Jr.
Deep Drilling in Crystalline Bedrock, Vol. 1: The Deep Gas Drilling in the
Siljan Impact Structure, Sweden and Astroblemes, A. Boden and K. G.
Eriksson, eds., Springer-Verlag, New York, 1988, pp. 148–155

FERMI NATIONAL ACCELERATOR LABORATORY: STANKA JOVANOVIC CURRICULUM VITAE
APRIL 1996

EDUCATION
B.S. Metallurgy—University of Belgrade. *1956*
M.S. Physical Chemistry—University of Chicago. *1958*

POSITIONS HELD
Retired. *May 31, 1996*
Senior Staff, Education Office, Fermi National Accelerator Laboratory.
1995–1996
Manager, Education Office, Fermi National Accelerator Laboratory.
1989–1995
President and Executive Director of Friends of Fermilab Association.
1983–1996
Chemist, Consultant and Special Appointee, Argonne National Laboratory.
1965–1989
Graduate Research Chemist, University of California, San Diego.
1960–1962
Metallographer, University of Chicago. *1958–1960*

SCIENCE EDUCATION RELATED ACTIVITIES
Organizer of the Needs Assessment Workshop for the Summer Institute for Science Teachers at Fermilab. *1982*

Organizer of the Needs Assessment workshop for Junior/Middle School Programs at Fermilab. *1983*

Organizer and member of the Curriculum Design Workshop for the Illinois Mathematics and Science Academy (IMSA). *1983*

Member of IMSA Program Planning Committee. *1986*

Member of the Organizing Committee of the 1986 Conference on the Teaching of Modern Physics at Fermilab. *1985–1986*

Organizer of the Needs Assessment Workshop for the Science Education Center at Fermilab. *1987*

Organizer and director of the Mini-Course on the Teaching of Modern Physics held in Mexico City, Mexico. *July 17–18, 1987*

Member and Co-Chair of the Finance Committee, Department of Energy National Teacher Enhancement Project Working Group. *1987–1991*

Member of the Department of Energy Precollege program Coordinating Committee. *1988*

Member of the Design Workshop for the Teachers Academy for Math and Science in Chicago. *1990*

Organizer of the Conference for Illinois Teacher-Leaders in Mathematics, Science and Technology Education. *1992*

Organizer of the Technology in Education Needs Assessment Workshop. *1994*

Organizer of Science Education Research Program Design Workshop. *1994*

Organizer of the American Renaissance in Science Education Workshop. *1995*

Participation in numerous Conferences and Meetings related to Education Programs at DOE National Laboratories. *1983–1995*

Under the leadership of S. Jovanovic over $10,000,000 has been raised for education programs at Fermilab. *1983–1996*

PRESENTATIONS

"Organization and conduct of precollege education programs at Fermilab and Oak Ridge Associated Universities and Oak Ridge National Laboratory," S. Jovanovic. *May 1986*

"Precollege Programs at Fermilab," Corridor Industrial Group, Fermilab, S. Jovanovic. *February 1986*

"Education programs at a Single Mission National Laboratory: Funding Needs," DOE-NSF initial meeting on the proposed interagency agreement for cooperative funding of education programs at national laboratories, Washington, D.C.. S. Jovanovic. *May 1987*

Member, panel on Education System, Federal Laboratory Consortium semi-annual meeting, Sacramento, California. *November 3–5,1987*

"Precollege Education Programs at Fermi National Accelerator Laboratory," Federal Laboratory Consortium semi-annual meeting, Session 1: Education System, Sacramento, California. S. Jovanovic. *November 3–5, 1987*

"Precollege Education Programs at Department of Energy National Laboratories," Department of Education National Title II Steering Committee Meeting, Washington, D.C.. *April 24, 1988*

"Precollege programs at Fermilab, DOE Honors Program and Summer Institute for Science and Mathematics Teachers," Idaho National Engineering Laboratory, Idaho Falls, Idaho. S. Jovanovic. *December 2, 1988*

Numerous presentations to internal and external Fermilab and Department of Energy Review Committees.

PUBLICATIONS

"1983 Summer Institute for Science Teachers," M. Bardeen, M. Cox, C. Hill and S. Jovanovic Fermilab Report, pp. 5–11 November 1983.

"1986 Conference on the Teaching of Modem Physics," S. Jovanovic Fermilab Report, pp. 1–8, April–May 1986.

"Fermilab Sponsors a Mini-Course in Mexico City on the Teaching of Modern Physics," S. Jovanovic Fermilab Report, pp. 2–6, July/August 1987.

"Precollege Education Programs at Fermi National Accelerator Laboratory," Stanka Jovanovic Fermi Report, pp. 21–25, November/December 1987 Author and co-author/editor of numerous grant proposals, program reports, How-to manuals, program guides and program brochures.

OTHER PROFESSIONAL PUBLICATIONS

Stanka Jovanovic is a chemist with over thirty years in geoscience research. She has worked with Cyril Stanley Smith at University of Chicago, Harold C. Urey at University of California, San Diego, and with George W. Reed at Argonne National Laboratory. Jovanovic has coauthored over fifty publications in open literature (list available at request) and numerous other technical reports and proposals.

COMMUNITY SERVICE

Founder and First President, Friends of Fermilab, Batavia, IL. *1983–1996* Board Member. *1983–present*

In May 1981, Leon M. Lederman, then Fermilab Director, invited Stanka Jovanovic to organize Friends of Fermilab, a not-for-profit corporation whose sole purpose is to provide support for precollege science education programs at Fermilab. It took two years and several other volunteers to design, organize, and legalize Friends of Fermilab. The first program, Summer Institute for Science Teachers, was conducted in 1983. Under Ms. Jovanovic leadership as the President of Friends of Fermilab and the Manager of Fermilab Education Office (established in 1989) the Leon M. Lederman Science Education Center, a facility dedicated to precollege programs, was designed, constructed and opened in 1992. Over the past thirteen years thousands of K-12 students and teachers participated in Fermilab programs.

Founder and first President, Junior Music Association of Downers Grove, IL. *1978–82*

Due to several referendum failures, all Downers Grove School District 58 extracurricular activities were eliminated in 1978, including the instrumental music program. Stanka Jovanovic organized a grass-roots movement that lead to the formation of a not-for-profit corporation with the sole purpose to provide instrumental music program for the District. Under a contractual agreement between the School Board and the Junior Music Association, on one hand, and between the Association and a instrumental music instruction provider, on the other, a tuition-based instrumental music program was offered to students in ten elementary and two Junior High School Schools in the District. Over 500 students participated annually in the program from 1978 to 1983. The District reinstated the program in 1983 and the Association dissolved after preserving the instrumental music education and serving the community well for five years.

YWCA of Metropolitan Chicago Forest Beach Camp Committee member. *1980–1985*

As the Committee member, Stanka Jovanovic mounted a major effort to prevent the sale of the 64-acre YWCA campsite on the shores of Lake Michigan, in New Buffalo, Michigan. In spite of the overwhelming need to preserve this unique sanctuary for generations of Chicago inner-city youth and their families, the Board of Directors of the YWCA of Metropolitan Chicago sold the camp. The loss was great, but equally great was the experience Stanka Jovanovic gained that served her well in her other community endeavors.

HIGH ENERGY
A Woman of Irresistable Force Battles for Science Education
By Mary Peterson Kauffold, Photo by Mario Petitti

Somewhere between huddling with her grandmother in the basement of a Yugoslav apartment building during World War II as American planes rained bombs overhead and analyzing Apollo mission moon rocks at Argonne National Laboratory, Stanka Jovanovic discovered freedom.

It was a quest well worth the undertaking, she says. Along the way, she learned the antithesis of life isn't death. It's the absence of freedom.

Only 12 at the time of the American shelling, Jovanovic vividly recalls that for three hours she didn't know if the blast that had leveled the top two stories of her Belgrade home also had sealed off her underground sanctuary, turning it into a tomb. Ironically, 13 years later, the same country that sent the bombs, would deliver her from Communist controlled Yugoslavia. The United States of America liberated Stanka Jovanovic, now 57. And she never forgets a favor.

It's payback time.

Because she believes the real currency of democracy is education, Jovanovic is settling her debt by creating new opportunities for learning that promise to pay big dividends for generations to come. She is a driven broker of dreams, self energized beyond reason, with a passion for molding the possible into the real.

"Stanka is an irresistible force, as we say in physics," says 1988 Nobel laureate Leon Lederman, who, as director of Fermi National Accelerator Laboratory in Batavia, abandoned his meditations on elementary (sub-atomic) particle physics long enough to recruit Jovanovic in 1982 for a special mission. Her marching orders were to amass the considerable people and money necessary to make the lab a science education resource center for teachers and their pre-college students.

Why Jovanovic?

"Because she gets her way 99 percent of the time," Lederman says. And no one, not even him, is too important, too high-placed, too anything not to be collared by Jovanovic when she's under the influence of goal lust. "She'll barge in here no matter who I'm with," he declares. "If (former President) Reagan were in here, she'd still walk in, although she might say 'Excuse me' before she started talking. Then again, she might not bother to say 'Excuse me.'"

That kind of persistence is exactly what makes Jovanovic Lederman's kind of colleague. He says in earnest: "I could use a dozen Stankas. She has tremendous energy and enthusiasm. And she's competent." In short, she gets the job done. Jobs like founding Friends of Fermilab Association (FFLA) and serving as president and executive director. Jobs like raising about $2 million in membership subscriptions, grants and donations to pay for FFLA projects including seminars, student honors programs and special lectures that have touched more than 50,000 students (from kindergarten through 12th grade), and 6,000 teachers.

When asked to name a site at Frmilab that would be appropriate as a backdrop for a photo of Jovanovic, Lederman doesn't hesitate "Put her in front of one of our monster machines. We have some incredible machines here." Pick a big machine, one that's loaded with energy, he advises, suggesting the result would be a two-of-a-kind portrait.

Stanka's husband of 34 years, Fermilab senior physicist Drasko Jovanovic, has returned early from Northwestern University, and is told of Lederman's suggestion. Drasko says follow him. He knows just the right place for the picture. Drasko persuades Stanka to get up close but not too personal ("don't touch!" he barks), with the lab's Cockcroft-Walton pre-accelerator, which can zap 750,000 volts of electricity at whatever gets in the way. The machine is the first stage of a process that keeps Femilab scientists on the brink of cracking cosmic mysteries.

While Stanka poses, Drasko, 58, consents to being questioned about their private life. They met when Stanka was senior in high school. Drasko showed up as a stand-in lecturer for his father, Dragoljub Jovanovic, then a renowned Yugoslav physicist who had studied under and worked with Marie Curie (the Nobel laureate in chemistry and physics who discovered radium).

Drasko's relationship with Stanka blossomed at the University of Belgrade as they both pursued baccalaureate degrees, he in physics, she in metallurgy. "He was impressed with me," Stanka says. "I was a woman scientist. That was a rarity then."

It's true, Drasko admits, "I had an awe for women scientists, but recognize that I got it from my father because of his work with the distinguished Madam Curie." The clincher to the romance had little to do with academic-related turn-ons, though. Young Stanka was no shrinking violet when it came to a little adventure. "She climbed mountains with me," Drasko says.

"Hike mountains," Stanka corrects. "Climbing means something different here. We hiked up mountains."

Okay, he says, they hiked mountains. More important, they still do, from their getaway home near the Teton Mountain range. In the next 20 years, he says, "if I can get her to go sailing, that would be perfect. She wants to stay on the beach, but I want to be in the boat."

Without missing a beat, Stanka shoots back, "If he learns how to sail, probably I'll go."

Their bunter is littered with a mix of mischief and affection. Life with Stanka, Drasko decrees, "is never boring."

In a more reflective mood, Drasko says part of his wife's charm as a companion and friend is her complete honesty: "There isn't a thought so bad she wouldn't tell me. It's a great advantage when you don't ever have to second guess someone." What makes him most sad is the thought "that she might go [die] before me."

When she came to the U.S. in 1956, Stanka had no intention of staying. She came to study because Drasko had received a fellowship at the University of Chicago. They'd been married only a month before he departed, and at the time of Stanka's arrival, had been separated for two years.

When Drasko greeted her with the announcement that they weren't retuning to Yugoslavia, Stanka was shocked. They had an argument. She wasn't about to stay in America so they could have a few more material things "like a TV and a refrigerator," she told him firmly. He counseled her to wait and see how she felt after living here awhile.

A short time later, a fat envelope arrived in the mail with college club information. The cover letter instructed her to select the student groups she'd like to join. Stanka was devastated. "Not here too," she remembers thinking. Back home, student organizations were all political. Choosing not to belong was enormously costly in lost job and educational opportunities. When Drasko and a friend assured her that that wasn't how things worked here—she would be judged on the basis of her good science, not her political persuasion—she could hardly believe it. Stanka suddenly developed an insatiable appetite for personal freedom. She became a U.S. citizen in 1965. She and Drasko have lived in Downers Grove since 1966.

Things might have turned out better though, better for Stanka anyway, Drasko allows, if she were starting her career today: "If she had grown up in America, she could have been a very successful corporate director or a very successful business woman making very good money.

"Stanka is very generous. She sacrificed her career to bring our family up. She kept a comfortable home and focused on me and my career. Her career was not as important." He looks somber and stares at the floor. "We're the old generation. We didn't start our careers with the idea of equal opportunity for men and women. Today, I would wait for her to get her doctorate." (They both did their graduate work at the University of Chicago. Stanka received a master's degree in chemistry in 1958. A year later, Drasko received a doctorate in physics.)

Stanka is a gifted research chemist, according to her collaborator of more than two decades, Argonne's chemist George Reed. From the start, he respected Stanka's decision to work part-time, on a flex-time basis as a special consultant. "She had a family and home to take care of, and she wasn't interested in working full-time," Reed said, adding that having Stanka as a partner is well worth any inconvenience her schedule may cause. Her keen insight into research problems, organization skills and training make her part-time work "almost equal to full time for any normal person," he said.

Without question, Stanka's first priority was the raising of her daughters, Jasna, 25, and Vesna, 21. "As a mother, she's a tigress,' Drasko says. "Touch one of her daughters, and you'll get your eyes scratched out. When she found out the younger daughter couldn't get her music [lessons] at school, by God, she set out to change the world!" And in the process, she changed the course of her life.

It happened in 1978. Vesna, then in fifth grade, was a drummer in the school band. Stanka remembers being furious when her youngest child came home complaining that the band program was slated to be axed, a victim of budget cutting. "Well, who's going to do something about this," she wondered.

The school principal told Stanka to take her complaint to the school board. She had no idea what that meant. Up to then, she'd been a quiet homemaker and a happy scientist who minded her own business. Conditioned to live by the don't-bother-anyone-who isn't-bothering-you dictum for survival she learned under Communist role, Stanka's political comfort zone was non-existent. Authority was something to be respected, not questioned.

"I was totally shocked that the Department of Education was not [prescribing] the curriculum.... I was surprised I could do something about education," she recalls.

Jovanovic attended her first school board meeting. She says she had zero concept of what was going on, but she was determined Vesna would have the chance to study music; so she mustered her courage and asked the superintendent if he would seriously consider a proposal that would pay for the program, not out of tax dollars, but some other way. Of course, he said.

A self-described catalyst, she quickly attracted a group of interested parents and community leaders. They named Jovanovic the founder and president of the new Junior Music Association of Downers Grove. One day, while driving past a group of children waiting at a school bus stop with their instruments in tow, the magnitude of what had been accomplished hit her. "My God, it's us that did that," she remembers thinking. She felt empowered by democratic freedoms that she never really understood before. For five years, the association provided 500 children in 10 elementary and 2 junior high schools with access to a school band and orchestra.

The program funding was put back into the school budget in 1983.

Vesna's and Jasna's descriptions of Stanka's talents as a mother paint her in shades of Super Mom, To put it simply, they said, their mother has been, is now and always will be their best friend. They wouldn't think of going a day without talking with her at least once—for advice, for fun, for commiseration or just to suggest a TV program for viewing that night. With both daughters scattered around the country, phone bills of $400 to $500 are common. Stanka picks up the tab.

Stanka says her daughters are her greatest success. She raised them to believe without question that they were the equal of men and capable of achieving any goal they set for themselves. "I was shocked when I went out into the world and saw sexism," said Vesna, who smiled unselfconsciously when she introduced herself as Stanka's baby. Home for a visit after graduating last month from New York University Tisch School of the Arts, Vesna was preparing to leave for Los Angeles and a career in film production.

Jasna and Vesna believe their mother wanted to create the secure, happy childhood and close-knit family she never had. Stanka's parents divorced at an early age, and aunts and her grandmother raised her. Her childhood memories are scarred with wartime recollections of Nazi atrocities.

"Jasna and I are the most important people in the world to my mother," Vesna declared. "In our family, we tell each other 'I love you' 25 times a day, and when we're together we hug each other all the time. It's something I'll be able to give back to my children someday."

Jasna, who is working on a doctorate in human development and family studies at Pennsylvania State University, recently studied for several months at the University of Belgrade, her parents' alma mater. She said being in the city at the same age Stanka was when she came to the U.S. made her appreciate how difficult it must have been for her mother to leave her home. Jasna said she now realizes that she and her sister are beneficiaries of that decision.

Considering her mother's troubled childhood, Jasna said she's surprised that Stanka didn't chose to be a little more selfish with her time and wealth. But that's not her mother's way, she said. Stanka is dedicated to helping others learn how to better themselves. "If someone came to her starving to death, she'd feed them, of course," Jasna explained, "and then she'd get them a job or put them in school."

Stanka is about to begin the second chapter in her life's work. When Reed retires soon from Argonne, she has decided that she, too, will leave to devote her time to what she calls the logical next step in FFLA activities: FermiCenter, a planned 12,000 square-foot hands-on science center.

Marjorie Bardeen, vice president of FFLA, who oversees the association's curriculum programming, boasted that when the center's doors open, hopefully in the fall of 1990, it will house a visitors hall with 20 to 30 interactive displays, classrooms, an auditorium and a collection of instructional materials for school teachers including a database linked to a telephone hot-line.

It's imperative that projects like FermiCenter must be nurtured and supported by the American people, Jovanovic insists, because education is the basis for all freedom, especially science education: "By the 21st Century, we will have to be scientifically literate because we'll be voting on critical issues that are tied to technology. That's especially important in this country where people make the choices rather than the government making the choices.

"Anyone who is scientifically illiterate will lose the chance to practice good decision making." And that, she says, is the essence of freedom.

BOOKS PUBLISHED BY STANKA JOVANOVIC

My Life from Yugoslavia to America, 2005, DJ Publishing, Urbana, Illinois

Dimitrijevic Family Genealogy, 2005, DJ Publishing, Urbana, Illinois

My Family, Irma Mackin as told to Stanka Jovanovic, 2005, DJ Publishing, Urbana, Illinois

Yugo Reunions 1956–2003, Eleven Friends and Their Life Stories, 2006, DJ Publishing, Urbana, Illinois

Trbojevic Family Genealogy, 2008, DJ Publishing, Portland, Oregon